D0935545

FEARLESS
LEADERSHIP

FEARLESS LEADERSHIP

Overcoming Reticence, Procrastination,
and the Voices of Doubt Inside Your Head

ALAN WEISS, PhD

First edition published in 2020

by Routledge/Bibliomotion, Inc.
52 Vanderbilt Avenuve, 11th Floor New York, NY 10017
2 Park Square, Milton Park, Abingdon, Oxon OX14 4RN, UK

© 2020 by Alan Weiss
Routledge/Bibliomotion is an imprint of Taylor & Francis Group, an Informa business

No claim to original U.S. Government works

Printed on acid-free paper

International Standard Book Number-13: 978-0-367-33736-0 (Hardback)

This book contains information obtained from authentic and highly regarded sources. Reasonable efforts have been made to publish reliable data and information, but the author and publisher cannot assume responsibility for the validity of all materials or the consequences of their use. The authors and publishers have attempted to trace the copyright holders of all material reproduced in this publication and apologize to copyright holders if permission to publish in this form has not been obtained. If any copyright material has not been acknowledged please write and let us know so we may rectify in any future reprint.

Except as permitted under U.S. Copyright Law, no part of this book may be reprinted, reproduced, transmitted, or utilized in any form by any electronic, mechanical, or other means, now known or hereafter invented, including photocopying, microfilming, and recording, or in any information storage or retrieval system, without written permission from the publishers.

For permission to photocopy or use material electronically from this work, please access www.copyright.com (http://www.copyright.com/) or contact the Copyright Clearance Center, Inc. (CCC), 222 Rosewood Drive, Danvers, MA 01923, 978-750-8400. CCC is a not-for-profit organization that provides licenses and registration for a variety of users. For organizations that have been granted a photocopy license by the CCC, a separate system of payment has been arranged.

Trademark Notice: Product or corporate names may be trademarks or registered trademarks, and are used only for identification and explanation without intent to infringe.

Library of Congress Cataloging-in-Publication Data

Names: Weiss, Alan, 1946- author.
Title: Fearless leadership : overcoming reticence, procrastination, and the voices of doubt inside your head / Alan Weiss.
Description: 1 Edition. | New York : Routledge, 2020. | Includes bibliographical references and index.
Identifiers: LCCN 2019036248 (print) | LCCN 2019036249 (ebook) | ISBN 9780367337360 (hardcover) | ISBN 9780429322006 (ebook)
Subjects: LCSH: Leadership.
Classification: LCC HD57.7 .W45188 2020 (print) | LCC HD57.7 (ebook) | DDC 658.4/092--dc23
LC record available at https://lccn.loc.gov/2019036248
LC ebook record available at https://lccn.loc.gov/2019036249

Visit the Taylor & Francis Web site at
http://www.taylorandfrancis.com

To all those dogs who have lived with us and who have immeasurably brightened every day, been my therapy, and chased a ball and ran through a gate with unrestrained vigor: Buck, Trotsky, Phoebe, Koufax, Buddy Beagle, Bentley, and Coco.

I've loved you all, and I'm glad you all receive a guarantee of heaven.

Yea, though I walk through the valley of the shadow of death, I will fear no evil.
—*23rd Psalm*

Contents

Other Works by Alan Weiss

Alan Weiss on Consulting (interviewed by Linda Henman, Aviv Shahar)
Best Laid Plans (originally *Making It Work*)
Getting Started in Consulting (also in Chinese)
Good Enough Isn't Enough (also in Spanish)
Great Consulting Challenges
How to Acquire Clients
How to Establish a Unique Brand in the Consulting Profession
How to Market, Brand, and Sell Professional Services
How to Sell New Business and Expand Existing Business
How to Write a Proposal That's Accepted Every Time
Life Balance
Lifestorming (with Marshall Goldsmith) (also in Korean, Indonesian, Turkish)
Managing for Peak Performance (also in German)
Million Dollar Coaching (also in Portuguese)
Million Dollar Consulting (also in Portuguese, Russian, Polish, Chinese, Korean, Arabic)
Million Dollar Consulting Proposals
Million Dollar Consulting® Toolkit
Million Dollar Launch
Million Dollar Maverick
Million Dollar Referrals
Million Dollar Speaking (also in Chinese, Portuguese)
Million Dollar Web Presence

Money Talks (also in Chinese)
Organizational Consulting
Our Emperors Have No Clothes
Process Consulting
The Business Wealth Builders (with Phil Symchych)
The Consulting Bible (also in Portuguese)
The DNA of Leadership (with Myron Beard)
The Global Consultant (with Omar Kahn)
The Great Big Book of Process Visuals
The Innovation Formula (with Mike Robert) (also in German, Italian)
The Language of Success (with Kim Wilkerson)
The Resilience Advantage (with Richard Citrin)
The Son of the Great Big Book of Process Visuals
The Talent Advantage (with Nancy MacKay)
The Ultimate Consultant
The Unofficial Guide to Power Management
The Power of Strategic Commitment (with Josh Leibner and Gershon Mader)
Threescore and More
Thrive!
Value-Based Fees
Who's Got Your Back? (with Omar Khan)

Acknowledgments

Business executives and entrepreneurs have been trusting me for 30 years and I've tried to live up to their expectations. My thanks to every one of them who chose to work with me.

Thanks to my wife, Maria, and the entire family for indulging me in my idiosyncratic and peculiar career: Danielle, Jason, Gabrielle, Alaina, Jan, and Grace.

Introduction

My father was a paratrooper at the outset of World War II and jumped from low-flying cargo planes into enemy guns over the jungles of New Guinea. A lot of men in his unit never made it home.

He seldom talked about the war, but one day when I asked him, "What about the fear?" he said, "I just assumed it would never be me." He passed away in 2016 at the age of 99 years and 11 months.

No one is shooting at us, yet our fears are often far worse than those of people in combat, of people in harm's way, of police officers pursuing assailants or firefighters running into burning buildings. We equate fearlessness with rashness, but in reality, we're scared over nothing at all. Yet this programmed fear dilutes our efforts, undermines our talents, and reduces the results in both our personal and professional lives.

It also ruins relationships.

I've coached top executives and entrepreneurs globally for over 30 years. Sometimes I feel like a lion tamer with a chair and a whip entering the cage, yet most of the time I've found pussycats. I know there are exceptions: Jack Welch (GE) and Steve Jobs (Apple), Herb Kelleher (Southwest Airlines) and Fred Smith (FedEx). But they are far outnumbered by the highly paid, highly situated executives who have asked me before they allow our time together to end, with massive insecurity, "Could I make it in your other major clients?"

Say, what?

I've seen entrepreneurs with great ideas and huge energy crumble with potential investors, bankers, and partners because they are more afraid of rejection than they are proud of their innovation. They don't fear gambling with the family home, but they do fear their ego being bruised.

In sports, the offense wins points and the people on the offense who yell for the ball are the ones who score, not those trying to avoid the pressure shot, the clutch play.

My intent in this book—my goal for you—is to understand the baseless underpinnings of almost all of our fears. You read that correctly, *almost all* of our fears, and therefore to discard them. I've educated and coached people in the discovery of, examination of, elimination of, and sustained freedom from fears.

We all know people who are charming and articulate, but flounder on a stage addressing colleagues; musicians who master intricate scores but can't play the basics when asked to solo; athletes who "choke" when the game is on the line; business people who are strong until it comes time to ask for the business; people who consistently feel like "imposters."

We are far better at dealing with external, tangible fears than our own imagined ones. We purchase insurance, watch the safety demonstrations, know how to use the Heimlich Maneuver. But those are responses to rare and often never-occurring emergencies. (The great preponderance of police officers never draw their guns in the line of duty through their entire careers.) Our mythical and monstrous fears are daily dark clouds, masking our talents no less than depression or guilt.

It's time to realize there is no monster under the bed, never has been and never will be, *without having to check nightly and without needing a weapon on the night table.* Picture yourself freed of restraints that you could never properly articulate and were loath to discuss, but which you carried on your shoulders constantly, a voice of doubt whispering in your ear, a dead weight, nonetheless.

It's time to stop slouching along the wall and start running down the street. We're going to face up to fears and then jettison them—lighten our load. Then there's no stopping you after that.

—**Alan Weiss**
East Greenwich, RI
December 2019

CHAPTER 1

Real Fear and Fraudulent Fear

We should fear certain events and circumstances, but they fall into clear categories and occurrences. Fear is somewhat infectious, in that once it's in our system it tends to take up residence and spread its tentacles into areas that are completely inappropriate. There's a metaphoric "guy on our shoulder" (the voice of doubt) whispering in our ear, "Be afraid, be very afraid."

The Tyrannosaurus and the Tyrant

That wonderful 100-million-year creation of the Jurassic and Cretaceous periods, the T-rex familiarly, is probably the fiercest carnivore and killing machine in history. Its size, enormous teeth, speed, and varied diet were the causes of its incredible longevity, ended only when a giant piece of space junk slammed into the Yucatan.

Modern recreations of the monster depict an agile, feather-covered predator which ruled absolutely. Not many of the young made it to adulthood, but those that did you could probably see growing in front of you, since in a relatively brief time they grew to about 15 tons. That's as much as ten Bentleys, more or less.

This animal is my starting point for several reasons. First, I want to point out that scientists who study predation have concluded that the success rate of predators—whether the T-rex, a pelican, or a cheetah (and excepting Wile E. Coyote)—was and is about one in ten. That is, they have to go on the attack about ten times in order to bring home dinner for the family.

Second, the T-rex was absolutely frightening, bellowing and screaming, immense, and quite fast.

Third, even the T-rex was helpless against that comet.

Leaders at all levels and people in varied pursuits tend to fear what they shouldn't (the customer or their own boss or speaking at a town meeting), not fear what they should (being left behind technologically or denying time with their family to work at their careers), and mistake what they can control and not control. The failure to deal successfully with ambiguity is a large part of fear, which we'll discuss later in the book.

We've seen T-rexes in leadership. I'd nominate the late Al Dunlop—"chainsaw Al"—who would cut everything possible in an organization to save money. I was once on a consulting assignment with Bill Klopman of Burlington Industries who would scream obscenities at his top executives and send them running from the room in the aftermath of his fury. Those of us who remember taking history courses when they were required in school remember Hitler and Stalin, Mao and Idi Amin. There are martinets in the arts, in non-profits, and in athletics.

You may be able to feed yourself through predation, but you can't lead. Tyrannosaurs didn't travel in packs, had no hierarchy, no corner offices. It was every reptile for itself.

So why is it that leaders feel threatened, frightened, and fearful? Why do the people in power with big teeth, a bellowing roar, and heavy weight often act (or fail to act) out of fear?

Here are the primary reasons:

1. Ego sensitivity. Our egos are often bolted to the front of the ship, absorbing the winds and waves and getting battered. Our ego should be down in the cargo hold, safely tucked away.

2. Ambiguity. We fear the unknown and see grey areas as potential traps instead of potential opportunity. After all, if you're not sure what's in the dark why assume that it's bad?

3. Lack of proportion. We tend to see victory as transient and defeat as inevitable, waiting just around the corner. We overstate risk and believe we'll have a hard time doing things *despite all evidence to the contrary!*

4. Poor and low self-esteem. Leaders often feel like imposters, uncertain as to how they've had the good fortune to arrive where they are and certain they'll be "found out." Almost every Oscar-winning actor you see at the ceremonies is worried about whether he or she will work again. After all, they've received awards for portraying someone who's not them.

Fear Factor

Our default position is to fear, and we have to change it. A question, objection, rebuttal, or adverse reaction are all signs of interest. It's apathy that's horrible, but confrontation is actually quite healthy.

When I first played Little League® baseball I drove myself into a panic. How could I hit a ball with a bat? Even though I had been practicing continually, there were adults looking on and I might let down my teammates. I was shaking when I reached the plate and struck out on three pitches. The pitcher wasn't very good. But I wasn't about to hit anything in my state of fear.

The same holds true for newly appointed leaders, or those who face a new scenario (addressing the media), or those who feel their entire careers are on the line (presenting to the board), or those who believe they've erred and failed (if you're not failing, you're not trying).

We encounter people who are afraid to make a decision, despite the urgency of the matter. We deal with people who procrastinate endlessly, less afraid of the criticism they receive for procrastination than the fear of making a decision or taking an action that's wrong. And then there are the perfectionists who refuse to move unless everything is exactly right—which it never will be. The "threshold effect" occurs when the temporary fear of doing something is outweighed by the long-term pain. So we go to the dentist, accepting short-term pain instead of permanent discomfort. The problem, of course, is that many people won't endure the pain of a divorce in the moment and instead lead a lifetime of loveless misery.

Perfectionism is the enemy of excellence and is generated by fear of being imperfect. Therefore, you'll never be excellent, either.

Finally, as a consultant and coach, I've encountered leaders all too often who are afraid of acting without the consensus—or, worse, uniformity—of their direct reports. They fear people "won't be on board," or will not fully commit, or will actually undermine the project or initiative.

This is an abdication of power and responsibility. I fondly recall the great scene from *Indiana Jones* where Harrison Ford is confronted by a warrior expertly swinging two horrible swords, one in each hand, and barring the way. Ford pulls out a gun and shoots him.

Now, I'm not advocating armed leadership. But I am suggesting it's folly to disregard the weapons at your disposal, especially when they can overcome those issues which create fear.

The T-rex had the jaw power to bite through a modern automobile, let alone the bones of its prey. It didn't need reminding of that, it instinctively knew it.

Fight, Flee, Fright

Psychologists talk about the "fight or flight" phenomenon (also known as acute stress response and labeled by Walter Cannon 100 years ago*). This can be triggered by a loud noise in the house at night or speaking to

---

* He was chairman of the psychology department at Harvard University and published *The Wisdom of the Body* in 1923 (current publisher W.W. Norton & Co.).

colleagues in a business meeting. The terror releases hormones that help deal with the threat.

Fighting or fleeing were the two options always recognized, but I'd like you to consider a third: fright. You might consider the fright something that triggers the other two options, but I've found it increasingly a third option that paralyzes leadership.

When we face these choices, we experience increases in blood pressure (which is why your pressure shoots up in the dentist's office), a faster heartbeat, and stressed breathing. The perceptions and connections here are key: We've all experienced these conditions simply seeing a police car suddenly appear on the side of the road even though we're not speeding or breaking any laws!

The positive side of all this is that you should be hormonally better prepared for the challenge ahead. You may prepare better for the presentation or run faster from the perceived mugger. However, these perceived threats and dangers—some real and some not so real because perception *is* reality— often paralyze us or cause false senses of threat. People develop phobias and have anxiety attacks in elevators, airplanes, and business meetings ("What if I'm called on to give an opinion?"). These conditions undermine performance and mask talent.

This is where my third option "fright" enters the picture. Fighting leads to direct confrontation, physically or rhetorically, and fleeing leads to a rapid departure from the threat. However, we're often stuck on the third rail, and we simply remain frightened, frozen in place, unable to move, or decide, or recover.

Many of the notorious corporate scandals were rooted in fright: the inability of people to counter the dysfunctional normative behavior around them to either depart or blow the whistle (flight or fight). At Volkswagen, there was active and passive participation in covering up their false emission standards claims. At Wells Fargo the same occurred with the fraudulent customer accounts that were opened and sustained. Enron collapsed because of these dynamics. The space shuttle *Challenger* crashed because engineers' warnings went unheeded or were overridden.

Frightened leadership is an organizational toxicity. As much as Mark Zuckerberg is a pioneer launching the now ubiquitous Facebook, he seems frightened about the legitimate uproar over lack of privacy and hateful language on the site. He's not running from it, but he's not fighting it, either. He seems caught in the headlights.

Fear Factor

The reason we talk about a "deer frozen in the headlights" is that the deer cannot fight a car and doesn't flee because it's too frightened by an unexpected threat. Usually, it is killed.

What are the elements that cause these reactions in leaders to go on the offensive, run away, or simply freeze in place? I think they include:

- Unexpected competitive moves in the marketplace.
- New technology with uncertainty about usefulness.
- Customer revolt over operations (e.g., sources of labor).
- Challenges to longstanding assumptions (e.g., demographic change).
- Unanticipated capacity demands.
- Departure of key talent.
- Media revelations (whether true or untrue).

I'm writing this chapter looking out over the New York City skyline. In the hundreds of buildings I can see are thousands of leaders making tens of thousands of decisions cumulatively every day, millions a year. Even if only one percent of them involve triggers to the fight/fright/flight dynamics, multiply that over a career (or lifetime) and you can begin to appreciate how important it is *to anticipate and regulate these responses, to avoid fright and rationally determine whether to fight or depart so that you can fight another day.*

Right now, too many leaders are not making any decisions at all because they are "caught in the headlights." And often their most trusted advisors are attorneys who are inculcated to be archly conservative and whose counsel is often to do as little as possible.*

The ancient Greeks believed that there was nothing more glorious than to die on the battlefield. The ancient Romans believed that when facing overwhelming odds you retreated in order to fight another day.

I'm a Roman in this regard.

Consider the times in your past when you faced a business or family decision, whether crisis and traumatic or commonplace and normal, and you made, in retrospect, the wrong decision. You ran when you should have fought, you fought when you should have run, you froze when you should have either run or fought.

Airline pilots are trained and inculcated to fight ("the right stuff") because the other options doom the plane. A "killer instinct" is desired in most sports and games, from chess to video games, from rugby to badminton.

Sears was an innovative pioneer, using catalogs on the early railroads opening up the West and creating brick and mortar stores that sold everything from insurance to lawnmowers, saws to tires. Why did Sears inexorably decline like the proverbial frog in the hot water, failing to adapt to the Internet? In fact, why wasn't it Sears which morphed into today's Amazon?

It's because the board and management froze and fled. They didn't fight. No one would ever accuse Sears of having fearless leadership.

Appropriate Actions Begin with Rational Beliefs

Our belief system determines our attitudes, which are, in turn, manifest in our behaviors (Figure 1.1).

---

* I've often claimed that the ideal advice from an attorney is simply not to open for business, to leave the doors locked and the lights off. That way, nothing bad could possibly happen!

Figure 1.1　*Beliefs to behaviors.*

We may believe, for example, that employees are expenses that need to be controlled. Our attitude would be that they are replaceable at cheaper cost and that we don't intend to pay much attention to attrition. Our resulting behaviors might include that I dine in the executive dining room and never in the cafeteria.

Conversely, if our belief is that employees are assets which must be nurtured and retained, our attitude would be that we must provide them with the best tools and methods for their performance and success. Thus, our behavior would be to interact with employees frequently to hear what they have to offer in terms of their needs.

We've all seen the signs on the walls of offices which state the organization's "beliefs," and the fourth one down is usually something like "People are our most important asset." Yet you see managers berating employees in front of the signs! (I asked a CEO client of mine who was having cognitive dissonance about this, "Bill, do you think people believe what they read on the walls or what they see in the halls?")

To be fearless in leadership means we need the correct set of beliefs and the empirical evidence to support them. For example, most people thought at one point that employees were simply motivated by money. But we now know that if you give an unhappy employee more money, *you merely have a wealthier, unhappy employee.*

We need to deconstruct our beliefs so that we're confident our consequent behaviors are best for fearless leadership. Here are some contrasts:

Paranoia	Health
• I can't allow subordinates to take credit	• Subordinates' success credits me
• I should stay off radar screens to survive	• I need to be in the spotlight to thrive
• Everyone is seeking my job	• I'm ready and able to move up
• Grooming a successor is dangerous	• Grooming a successor is the only way I can be freed for promotion
• My boss doesn't acknowledge my talent	• I'm going to demonstrate my talent widely and publicly
• I want to avoid conflict	• Healthy conflict moves us forward with more thorough insights
• I'm lucky I got here	• They're lucky I'm here
• I want to be perfect	• I want to be successful, which includes being resilient after errors
• I'm being critically viewed daily	• I welcome constructive feedback

There are quite a few people immersed in the left column of my chart. Note that it's not difficult to adjust your behaviors IF you are willing to change your mindset from the paranoid to the healthy.

When Eisenhower was faced with launching over a million troops on the last days the tides permitted that June in Normandy, and he had an uncertain weather report, he gave the order to go forward. He didn't seek guarantees (which were impossible), and didn't flee (retreat, which would have exposed the invasion strategy), but chose to fight.

Mike Tyson, the former heavyweight champion boxer, said once that we all have a plan entering the ring until we're punched in the jaw. After that, you simply fight as hard as you can.

The worst-led companies in the world are those which promote executives to top positions because those people have never taken risks, been in "trouble," or sparked controversy. The best-led companies are those with innovative, resilient, people promoted to top spots.

In my youth, I watched baseball legend Jackie Robinson steal home many times. It is extremely difficult to do, and virtually no one does it today. He did this 20 of 32 attempts in his career, a tad over 60 percent. (The overall percentage of *all stolen base*s today is under 70 percent.) He wasn't concerned about bad press if he were thrown out, nor about getting hurt, nor about getting hit with a bat or ball.

He took risks to help his team. He fought.

On the last day of the 1941 season, Ted Williams was asked by his manager if he'd like to sit out the game, because he had a .400 batting average at stake (he was the last one ever to do this, 80 years ago). Williams refused, saying he'd play, and he successfully hit that day to maintain his average.

Jack Welch proclaimed that every company GE owned had to be either number one or two in its respective market. The company grew tremendously profitable. But look at it today, with no such "fight" but rather more of an emphasis on executive perks. (Welch was once called "neutron Jack.")

No one is shooting at us. Freezing is not an option. Fearless leadership is about taking the battle to the other person, the other organization, and into the marketplace.

Fear Is a Learned Behavior

A "learned behavior" is one that develops as a result of experiences. These are the seatmates of innate behaviors, which are genetically present and need no training. Some behaviors, of course, are both.

I know what you're thinking: Fear is "hardwired" into our genetic makeup, an ongoing reality from the first humans who had to learn to run from danger. My smaller dog is innately frightened by sudden noises. My German Shepherd is merely inquisitive. He has less to be worried about, given the fact he can readily defend himself.

But in leadership almost all fears are learned unless you're intending to conduct meetings on a high wire, or while free climbing, or amidst a pride of lions. (Even my Shepherd would demur.) Leadership behaviors are learned, and we have to understand the causes.

A brief digression: We cannot create improved behavior *contingently*, that is, simply patching up leaks and putting on band aids. We have to prevent the fearful behavior in the future by eliminating the probable causes. The therapist's admonition to "face our fears" is really an attempt to find the cause of them.

Hence, what do we "learn" that would cause us to be fearful? I'll suggest some categories and possible causes:

1. Errors are fatal. When we're young we may get thrown off the team or benched for making an error during the game, and perhaps not chosen on a team for a future game. We may flunk a test at school and threaten our chances for promotion or scholarships. If we make an error on a date, we may lose the partner we're desperate to attract and hold onto.

   Thus, in leadership, it's all too easy to believe that an error may lead to our ouster, or loss of a spot in the succession planning ladder, or a decreased bonus, or even termination. We believe that errors are the end of the road rather than just a bump in the road.

2. Perfection is the norm. Did your parents ever question why you didn't get all A's instead of only two and the rest B's? Have you been in situations where people critiqued totally tangential elements, such as the food or the lighting? (People who complain about airline food make me giddy. Are you expecting a safe trip to your destination, or a culinary experience?)

   We sometimes agonize over whether we should have cited four or six points instead of five in our presentation, when the audience considers us the expert and will accept whatever number we give them! I heard a story once about a New England medical convention where the highest rated speaker of the convention never arrived because of illness.

3. Recovery is impossible. That embarrassing moment, the lost sale, the erroneous report can never be "undone," the bell can't be "un-rung." But that's not what resilience is about.

  Lincoln was elected President after numerous defeats for lower office, the US suffered major defeats in the Pacific at the outbreak of World War II, major organizations have reinvented themselves from the brink of bankruptcy to become leaders, and future Hall of Fame coach Bill Belichick of the New England Patriots had a lousy record as head coach of the Cleveland Browns. If we accept errors as fatal in all conditions, then we become highly fearful of them. If we know we can readily recover and embarrassment is transitory, we lose our fear.

4. Low self-esteem. We see ourselves as "imposters" who will be "found out" sooner or later. Dr. Pauline Clance wrote *The Imposter Phenomenon* in 1984 (Snapfinger Publishing) in which she reported that over 80 percent of the executives, entertainers, and sports figures who were interviewed felt like imposters.

  We don't feel "worthy" (although we may well be effective) and we're fearful of someday being "exposed" for the imposters that we believe we are. When I first began speaking as a keynoter at a very young age, I was afraid that the audience would realize I was only speaking about common sense and would throw me out once they caught on. Fifty years later they still haven't.

Fear Factor

There's a difference between being efficacious and feeling worthy. When you do things well and feel good about yourself, you're healthy. When you do things well but don't feel worthy, you see yourself as the imposter. (When you see yourself as very worthy but are ineffective, in Texas they call it, "Big hat, no cattle.")

Since most of our modern-day fear is not hardwired and innate but learned, we can "unlearn" it. You can begin that process now by asking yourself these questions when you feel fear in a business setting (and even most social settings):

- Have I or anyone else I know failed at this and recovered from it?
- What is there about my life and work that represents high worth under any conditions?
- How have people best recovered from errors, failures, and setbacks in similar conditions?
- How do I achieve success, not necessarily perfection?

Those answers will tell you that your fears are unfounded and/or over-wrought and you can face them and overcome them.

Right in that moment.

The Guy on Your Shoulder

I've decided not even to try to make this gender-neutral. "The person on your shoulder" doesn't do it for me, doesn't convey the wise guy giving you grief. So forgive my male bias in this instance.

There is an anthropomorphic little guy on many of our shoulders, from the downtrodden to the high and mighty. He whispers into your ear that you're not good enough, should feel guilty, don't deserve what you have, and that you should be fearful. Very fearful.

This guy is the cumulative manifestation of all the baggage you carry around. He is a product of your superego, that part of your mind which is semi-conscious, and super critical, reflecting standards learned from parents, teachers, and other symbols of authority in your life.

In other words, the people who have packed all that baggage you're lugging around.

The superego generates criticisms, prohibitions, and inhibitions which represent social standards being violated. This is the little guy insinuating that you're not as good as the others, that you really can't and shouldn't do what you intend, and that you're going to stick out in a crowd like some kind of lout.

The superego also creates an idealized self-image of aspirations, an image that you ought to attain. Here the guy is yelling, "You'll never make it acting like that," and "You're going in the wrong direction," and "Haven't you been listening to anyone trying to help you?!"

The little guy is not there to help you. And he is present at all social and economic levels.

Fear Factor

I was leaving the office of an excellent CEO who had asked me to coach him for three months. After my final, glowing report, he stopped me at the door and asked, "Do you think I could make it at Merck?" (one of my top clients at the time and "America's Most Admired Company" according to Fortune *Magazine's annual survey). His superego was doing him no favors.*

The superego develops during the first five years or so of growth in response to authority figures' punishment and reward. The child embraces and internalizes the parental (and others') standards due in no small part to a tropism to identify with the parental figures. The idea (ideal) of family within a surrounding society becomes paramount. Supposedly, this will control transgressions and abnormal behavior.

Violation of social standards produces guilt and anxiety and the need to atone (which we see in religious form in rites such as Yom Kippur and Catholic Confession—reconciliation). As young people continue to grow and develop, the superego embraces further role models and rules of a changing society.

And the guy on your shoulder becomes a royal pain in the ass.

The superego is balanced by the ego and the id, which we won't go into here. But it's the superego which produces this guy who creates fear in your ear. He's constantly admonishing you that you're not good enough, and that when you are good enough (you win or succeed) that you're not really worth it or are being arrogant about it.

Many years ago there was a Disney science fiction movie, I believe the first in technicolor, entitled *Forbidden Planet*. The crew of a spaceship encounter a mad doctor (of course) aided by Robbie the Robot. He created monsters which plagued the crew until it was finally revealed he was merely recreating their own psychological fears and worries.

In other words, he had co-opted the little guy on their shoulders.

Once they realized they actually had control of their own *bête noir*, they were able to eliminate the monsters.

I think you can see where this is going.

We all require baggage, but it must be baggage that we pack ourselves, not packed by authority figures in our youth and constantly reopened by the guy on our shoulder. And we can't just drop the baggage on the train, because it's still with us travelling as fast as we are. You need to throw the baggage off the train, and pack new stuff. Don't be afraid to kill a metaphoric cow in the countryside.

To put it another way, we need to flick the little guy off our shoulder, let him hit the wall and bounce on the floor, and then stomp him until he bleeds out. (Or we need to convert him, which I'll discuss in the final chapter.)

How do we flick him off our shoulders?

- Examine your belief system and ask yourself whether it still reflects who you are today.
- Articulate your fear and ask yourself why it's valid and what are its origins.
- Ask yourself if you're acting in such a way because you're afraid to let others down, especially others no longer in your life.
- Examine what you've always believed and ask if conditions today still warrant such beliefs.

If you think this is silly or superficial, think again. It's simple but not easy. Remember when you hesitated to let an entire hour pass before entering the water, lest you get cramps and drown after a meal? Someone would say, "It's only been 52 minutes." That seems incredibly dumb today, but it's one of those authority tenets that we didn't question.

We have similar issues about appearing arrogant, or disappointing others, or being selfish, that too often control our behavior today.

Real fear is facing a tornado, or an illness, or a mugger. Fraudulent fear is allowing the little guy on your shoulder to intimidate you with ancient dicta and youthful paradigms.

And focus on the fact that a great deal of fear is actually self-induced, and we'll be dealing with that in the chapters ahead.

CHAPTER 2

The Origins of Your Current Fears

Many of our fears, if told to us as those of someone else, would seem minor or even preposterous. But we have an emotional connection often generated in our nurturing (or lack of nurturing). We can get rid of it if we can recognize it.

What Your Parents Told You and Didn't Tell You

Your parents (usually) assured you that there were no monsters under the bed. If we had the courage to check with a flashlight, we didn't find any.

That doesn't mean there were never monsters under the bed. There really is no empirical evidence that you never slept over a monster a few inches below the mattress. Absence of evidence is not evidence of absence.

In 1938, fishermen found a strange fish in their net near the Comoros Islands. It looked primitive, even prehistoric. They saved it and took it to authorities, who took it to scientists, who discovered that it was a coelacanth, a fish first thought to have evolved *400 million years ago,* and was firmly believed to be extinct for millions of years.

Apparently, no one had told this branch of the coelacanths who were thriving at deep depths unmolested, unchanged, with an estimated lifespan of about 60 years.

Some years ago, in southeast Asia, a deer was sighted. The unusual aspect of the sighting is that no one had ever seen this type of deer before. It was a "new" species, a significant sized mammal, no one knew existed.

We bemoan the loss of species and extinctions, but we also haven't come close to discovering all the species around us, from the ocean depths to the mountain tops, from the deep forests to the barren deserts.

My point is that the world is full of unknowns. An architect named Max Frisch once observed that "Technology is only our way of organizing the universe so we don't have to try to understand it." If I asked you if you believe there was life elsewhere in the universe, you have only three answers:

1. No (which is mind-boggling, because we'd be alone in the cosmos)
2. Yes (which is mind-boggling because we may one day meet)
3. I don't know (which is mind-boggling because we have no idea whether we're the only life in existence)

All of these are somewhat fearsome, but we live with them, just as we live with plane crashes but still fly, and food poisoning but still eat, and floods but still build homes near the water, and so on, and on. Our parents were comfortable assuring us that there were no monsters under the beds because they had never seen one, either, but also told us never to run with a sharp stick or we'd poke our eye out, which no one ever recalled actually occurring anywhere.

They never really took time to tell us that nuclear war could annihilate us, or that the Cuban Missile Crisis was a hair's breadth from nuclear war, or that polio couldn't be prevented or cured prior to the invention of the vaccine. They didn't tell us that there were pedophiles in highly unlikely places.

In other words, they tried to assuage our more baseless fears while protecting us or insulating us (or insulating themselves) from real ones. And more than a few of our elders believed in the Loch Ness Monster or that dead aliens were kept by the air force in some desert hangar. Even today, a large part of the population believes in flying saucers, the paranormal, and psychics.

We maintain today certain beliefs and non-beliefs that are daunting. People say they have no religion and no faith, but driving at 70 miles per hour just a few yards behind the car in front of you and in front of the car behind you requires a great deal of faith! We believe we're safe on the streets, despite terrorists who drive cars into pedestrians. Like my father the paratrooper, who believed it could never be him, we fly in the face of plane crashes.

I flew on a 737 MAX just two months before the first of two of them crashed. I thought it was simply nice to be on a new airplane.

If our parents told us some things to prevent certain behaviors and withheld others so as not to make us fearful and paranoid, what does that say about our current behavior today? Were people who suspected something was wrong at Volkswagen or Wells Fargo told, "Don't worry, top management would never allow such things to go on, don't be afraid"? Were people heavily invested in Bernie Madoff, who couldn't believe the promised returns in such an economy telling themselves, "There may be something wrong, but with so many major investors there's nothing to fear"?

Remember the Great Recession when it was said some institutions were "too big to fail"?

What false beliefs—myths, really—are you believing, or creating, or perpetuating? Fearless leadership is about dispelling falsity and purging myths, not using them as reference points. Here are some examples which you need to contemplate:

- No one is silly enough to ever use a nuclear weapon.
- My company would never lie to the public.
- The customer is always right.
- Diversity is more important than always choosing top talent.
- We can always find more money, get more credit.
- There's nothing here that would justify a negative news story.
- We treat all people with respect and fairness.

The beliefs that companies print in the annual report and hang on the corporate walls are not necessarily the same as those which are *operating* beliefs and govern daily behavior. Those *operational beliefs governing daily behavior are the only ones that really matter.* The annual report merely gathers dust on a shelf.

Norms vs. Beliefs

Normative pressure is that urgency created by other people to conform to their demands. This pressure can be aggressive or passive.

Aggressive: "You don't want to be the only person preventing us from having 100 percent contributions to the charity campaign."

"Don't apply for the golf foursome, we have better players and we could win the championship if we have room for them to play."

Passive: Everyone is driving through a broken gate so that they don't have to pay the parking fee at the working automated gates.

Everyone is using a stolen test to prepare for the exam and you'll be in bad shape if you don't use it too, because the marking is on a bell curve.

Beliefs are those convictions which you hold to be true, whether you have empirical evidence (your dog will defend you against strangers but is gentle with the children) or simply certitude (there is an afterlife, there is a Loch Ness monster).

These are two of the origins of many of our fears. (We discussed earlier in "the threshold principle" how strong normative behaviors can overcome our belief systems.) Here are examples of norms which create fears when unexamined or not opposed:

- We'll be considered as tyrants (for women: "bitches") if we are tough with subordinates. We're faced regularly with human resources ideas about treating people well, laws that forbid certain actions (like rapid termination), religious maxims ("do unto others...."), and movements such as "servant leadership."
- We came up the hard way, so others should, too. No one deserves rapid advancement, you have to earn every rung on the ladder. This

is especially prevalent in professional services firms (law, accounting, consulting) where it's very difficult to make partner and, once you do, you're not very eager to make it any easier for others.

- Profit is king, and short-term, quarterly profit is the ace. Forget about investing in the long term, strive for immediate gratification and quick profits that will make the analysts happy and your bonus higher.
- You don't talk to anyone but peers. You give orders to direct reports, have filters between you and the employees and customers. You run the business but you're not "in" the business.
- Mitigate risk. Use the lawyers to help run the business. Don't do anything you could be remotely sued for, and favor conservatism, not innovation.

Here are some examples of beliefs which create fears when unexamined or not challenged:

- Being publicly coached is a sign of weakness. If I need help, I'll do it privately or simply use trial and error.
- No one can do it as well or as fast as I can, so the critical issues I'll have to resolve myself, because I can't trust others to do them as well.
- Money is the prime metric. My success should be measured in how much total compensation I can generate for myself.
- We need to reduce expenses to every extent we can, through technology, automation, staff reduction, moving operations offshore, and replacing higher paid people with lower paid people.
- I'm not here to have fun or enjoy myself, and I have to have a stern demeanor and tough profile to show I'm in charge.

You get my drift. These are *unexamined* beliefs and perceived norms. Thus, we become fearful when we see what we deem to be imposing risk, threatening young people demanding change, diminishing profits, unstable expenses, others taking more time than we would with a mission critical initiative.

Yet we all would probably agree that the best organizations and top people take prudent risk, innovate regularly, encourage younger people to contribute, invest for longer-term growth, believe in being good community citizens, and create equitable compensation systems.

Leaders need to frequently evaluate the norms that are influencing them (both aggressive and passive) and beliefs which they hold that are eventually manifest in their behaviors. This isn't a remedial action, but rather one that we should proactively perform.

I read of a study once that revealed that advertising firms actually had a lower opinion of themselves than did their clients! The repercussions of that wrong perception (belief) were reflected in lower fees than could have been charged, more service attention than was necessary, and far more *angst* and meetings than were appropriate.

Inappropriate beliefs and oppressive norms create the fears which mask talent and stymie innovation.

Fear Factor

Most companies and entrepreneurs spend far too much time trying not to lose business than trying to win business. That's because they fear rejection and consequently act tepidly—and lose the business anyway.

Here is how you can combat this:

- Use an informal advisory group outside of your company with whom you can reciprocate. Test each other's beliefs and susceptibility to norms.
- Hire a coach, which is a sign of strength, and challenge that person to challenge you about these issues.
- Seek therapy if you have beliefs ("I'm an imposter in this job") that you can't shake or mitigate yourself.

- Talk to your spouse, partner, or close friends about your responses to issues and examine whether you're making effective decisions or falling prey to external pressures.
- Write down your true beliefs and ask yourself if they reflect who you are today and what you do today.

In doing this you may just find that it's time to discard a great deal of baggage.

The Baggage That Must Be Discarded

We have to jettison the baggage that houses our fears (and often creates new ones). Let me start by talking about worst case.

Some fears and their causes are so deeply rooted that they require a therapeutic intervention. I'm a great believer in therapy and have undergone it several times. Most people think it's remedial, but it's also a catharsis, and also attendant to success. Strong people aren't threatened by anything that can help them, which is why they're fine using a coach.

The same should hold true for a therapist.

Our phobias and irrational fears are usually minor. We manage to go to the dentist and flick an insect off of our arm. However, when significant anxiety arises, then we're dealing with phobias.

A phobia is an irrational aversion which can be exemplified by a fear of heights, public speaking, claustrophobia, sitting in the passenger seat or rear of a car, seeing blood, dealing with the board, facing conflict, and so forth. They are very often part of that baggage we have to jettison, but they can also develop late in life as you take on new jobs, experience an empty nest, get divorced, recover from illness, and experience similar major changes and trauma.

People often go to extremes to avoid irrational fears, such as avoiding an elevator that's already occupied, washing scores of times a day, refusing to talk to people who are suspected of disagreeing with them, and avoiding performance evaluations.

The first rational act is to recognize the irrational fear. (We talked earlier about many fears being rational and legitimate.) That's because they result in irrational actions which undermine you and your job. You may refuse to see your child's soccer game because you may encounter someone's dog there, and you may refuse needed medical treatments because you're terrified of test results. At work you might avoid meetings which will probably include argument and debate, or refuse to make demands about your compensation or working conditions.

Many people exhibit these physical symptoms when the stress level builds to a panic attack, for example, when being forced to speak publicly when such speaking is terrifying:

- Overwhelming perspiration
- Stomach and digestive discomfort
- Physical shaking
- Increased heart beat
- Chest pains
- Hot flashes and dizziness

Obviously, these can fatally undermine your efforts and influence as they are often uncontrollable. Thus, the second step after identification is to seek help if the symptoms persist, if they are causing you to change your schedules and appointments, and if you are unable to perform well due to them.

By starting with this "worst case" I'm strongly advising that you honestly evaluate your situation given these criteria and seek professional—clinical—help—to eliminate or at least mitigate these problems. You can usually begin with your personal physician, who knows you well, and ask for a referral to a good clinical psychologist (not a "life coach"!). You can also ask for suggestions from the American Psychological Association. (This is their Psychology Help Center: https://www.apa.org/helpcenter.)

Now for the "not worst case": self-help.

You can deal with your fears under certain circumstances. Here are some steps:

Face the fears candidly: Easier said than done, I know, but it's vital. Gradually allow yourself to be in the presence of the fear. Take a brief airplane trip, make a brief speech. Have a quick blood test, conduct a brief debate with a colleague.

Use a priority approach: Choose those fears which are *most* debilitating and cause you the most pain or deleterious effects. Not being comfortable addressing a board is far more important than being uncomfortable giving someone else negative feedback.

Break down the approach: Start by speaking to a single board member, then a group of three, then the entire board. Build your tolerance and your successes.

Reinforce: Remind yourself of what you've accomplished and keep doing it until it's no longer a fear requiring special attention but just another facet of your job.

Fear Factor

Overcoming a fear once doesn't really eliminate it. You need to constantly engage in the behavior to build it into your unconscious competency so that you can move on to other things.

Leaders are often susceptible to these irrational fears because they are thrust into positions of huge accountability, often without appropriate support. Former colleagues become subordinates, former superiors become peers, and a new set of superiors suddenly looms. The same occurs with a new initiative, or a new technology, or a new market.

When overwhelmed by a new situation or position, breathe deeply and slowly. Keep doing that until you feel calm and the symptoms we talked about above disappear. Listen to something soothing, such as music or a sound machine. Stand or sit straight, don't slouch. Engage in an activity you enjoy, whether at work or at home, that's appropriate.

We're all "thrown" by certain turns of events. The key is not to allow them to evoke or cause irrational fears. And you need to be very careful about your sources of information. Some people inadvertently trigger fears, and some are focused on making sure they do so.

Who the Hell Are You Listening To?

Chicken Little has come to rule the roost!

We may be, as I write this, in the longest growth period on record, but "a recession is coming." The team is good, but it can't win forever (although, for example, the New England Patriots usually do). Housing starts are up, but there's underlying weakness. Really? Where?

I remember the late Buddy Cianci, the longest serving mayor (of Providence, RI) in the country, who had an ongoing feud with the *Providence Journal*. "If I walked across the surface of the river tonight," he'd say, "the headline in the *Journal* tomorrow would be: Mayor Can't Swim!"

In the traditional planning processes in organizations, the dynamic works from the bottom up. (And strategy should work from the top down, which is why "strategic planning" is at least an oxymoron and at most meaningless.) The sales people low-ball their expectations in order to collect bonuses by exceeding their quotas, their sales managers further dilute the projections in order to protect themselves, and by the time all these numbers percolate up to senior management you have an anemic two percent growth projected and executives' hands are tied in terms of expansion and new investments.

However, fearless leaders simply ignore that system and assign the growth numbers needed for the company's strategy. When Steve Jobs regularly did this at Apple, it became known as "reality distortion." But Jobs's intent was accomplished most of the time, so I think it was more of "reality insertion" than "disruption." Jack Welch, while CEO of the GE conglomerate, with products ranging from light bulbs to locomotives, credit operations to network television, proclaimed, "We're going to be number 1 or number 2 in every market we enter or we will sell that business." Under his reign, GE was fantastically successful.

Fear Factor

Fearless leaders have to ignore the rubrics and patent medicine sold by human resources and a variety of consultants and trainers, who would maintain that "servant leadership" and "meritocracy" and "open book management" are the way to lead. The way to lead is to inspire people (and investors) to follow you, not join a herd and try to move en masse.

Lawyers are inculcated and paid to be archly conservative. They may be fine with contracts and court battles, but they are terrible business advisors because they want all of us to fear every kind of risk, even those well worth taking.

Paul Revere *knew* the British were coming. Chicken Little was simply shouting that the sky was falling. To whom are you listening?

One of the strongest communications channels in organizations is the "grapevine," the informal, unsanctioned, but highly efficient relaying of rumor and truth interspersed. You can't listen to the grapevine. I call it "schoolyard nonsense." Whether you believe people are questioning your judgment or upset with your decisions, it doesn't matter. But if you're concerned about being viewed positively by the informal communications and fearful of criticism, you're not going to lead very effectively.

Another very poor source of information which creates fear is test results. Human resources is famous for introducing usually unvalidated test instruments and surveys which judge leaders on factors such as listening skills, patience, employee engagement, and so on. The great problem here is that you shouldn't be participating in a popularity contest.

I once worked for a major pharma firm where these surveys were electronically renewed each quarter, and the senior managers were obsessed with moving a 6.7 rating on "shows empathy" to a 6.9 by the next survey date. All of this was wasted time, and created fear about bonuses, repute, and even minor behavioral quirks.

A third area of communications fear is that of the bully. I know you might say it's hard to bully a superior, but many superiors are loath to take on bullies because the experience is distasteful and often the bully is a high producer. (And sometimes the bully is your boss.)

Bullies are driven by vast insecurity complexes. (Many were abused as children.) They seek to bring everyone down to their own perceived level of inferiority through belittling and scare tactics. Two examples:

1. Bill Klopman, whom I cited earlier, was CEO of Burlington Industries when I was assigned to help conduct a strategy program there. He was obscene and malicious, cursing out his senior team and often sending someone scurrying from the room to retrieve something as if they were children. These people took that treatment because they were inferiors. No strong person would accept such demeaning treatment and no strong leader would dish it out. Strong leaders have strong lieutenants, weak leaders have weak lieutenants.

2. I worked in a major pharma organization as a consultant asked to coach the son of one of the founders who sold to this larger company. The son ran roughshod over everyone, was mean and perverse, dressing down people in the halls, and needed to be removed. The president, who was my client, told me, "Well, that's just Ricky." I told him, "Well, your people think it's you."

   "How can that be?!" he shouted, "everyone knows I regard people highly."

"They all think that Ricky could never get away with this kind of behavior if you didn't support it, so that he's your surrogate. Pretty soon your board will find out about this."

Ricky was fired that week.

You need to be careful about the sources of your information and to whom you pay attention. You're there to lead, not to be loved, not to scare, and not to be scared.

CHAPTER 3

Manifestations of Fear

We think we're not afraid but we act as if we're afraid. Procrastination is the greater fear of being critiqued for what you've actually done trumping the lesser fear of being hounded for not doing anything at all. Vacillation is fear, so is a refusal to act.

Procrastination

Procrastination is the act of delaying something for no good reason. In Latin, *procrastinare* means "to put off until tomorrow." In Greek, *akrasia* means roughly doing something against our better judgment.

Procrastinating, no matter how we tend to rationalize it by saying "this isn't the best time," or "there are other priorities," or "the moon is not in the shadow of Aries," is self-inflicted misery. It's misery because we're aware of it, we know we're doing it, we know we'll be criticized for engaging in it.

We fear moving and we fear not moving. How's that for a stellar "Catch-22"?

This mixes the irrational and rational fears we've been examining. We rationally know it's irrational to procrastinate. Yet we're addicted as if we've opened a box of chocolate-covered pretzels.

Yet this isn't an illness or a sin. It's a result of poor self-worth and low esteem. We need to conquer these feelings to overcome the fears that create procrastination. We need to focus on our attitude at the moment, not the perceived unpleasantness or gargantuan nature of the task at hand. Our self-doubt and insecurities promote our irrational beliefs that what we do can't possibly be good enough and critique is inevitable. Thus, I'll take a beating for not moving rather than moving into deep trouble.

Then we start the doom loop of blaming ourselves still more, lowering our esteem still further, and delaying still longer. We have to escape from this mental set. Procrastination provides us with immediate gratification in escaping the perceived negative task or responsibility. We tend to engage in such behaviors repeatedly to gain that short-term benefit. So we don't have an event, but rather a way of life.

This way of life can produce great stress with consequent deleterious implications for health, repute, potential, and so forth. The momentary gratification gives way to longer-term discouragement (or even depression). So we procrastinate still more. Its analogy is drug addiction: We feel terrible once the drug wears off, so we take more of the drug to feel better, with the result we'll feel even worse.

There is a great deal of "presentism" today, whereby we use our current values and beliefs to critique and even try to alter the past. We tear down statues, rename schools, stop honoring certain traditional heroes. Presentism, however, also relates to focusing exclusively on present (short-term) needs over longer-term needs. We identify, of course, with who we are today, not who we'll be in the future. When we're under stress, we don't make long-term decisions at all (or at least not very well or easily).

Even though we rationally recognize that procrastinating will create still more stress, we're more focused on removing the *fear* in the present. We talked at the outset about the amygdala's role in such cognition. That fear is quite strong, strong enough to affect leaders in daily decision making on an ongoing basis. And we can't just tell ourselves, as we would hear in some Bob Newhart routine, to just "stop it"!

Once we realize that we're talking about emotions and not the actual tasks, we can reclaim some of our control. We need to attack the immediate gratification of procrastination with alternative, healthier gratifications. I've found that it's almost impossible to "coach" someone out of procrastination. Here are some steps to take:

1. Recognize your procrastination and "forgive yourself" as you would forgive yourself an error or mistake or unkind word.
2. Build your self-esteem by focusing on your accomplishments and contributions *on a daily basis.* I've achieved great results with people by simply teaching them to take a minute in the morning and a minute in the evening to review what positive things they've accomplished and plan to accomplish.
3. Go public. Help others hold you accountable for deadlines, results, commitments, and so on so that you realize your procrastination would be letting down others who are important to you. (And do the same for others.)

I don't mean to make this sound easy, I simply intend to explain that it's eminently possible.

On a more granular level, understand the components of what you want to accomplish, not merely the totality. Launching a new product is daunting, but finding a project manager, selecting a trial market, and agreeing on a price might be much more comfortable as component actions. Keep breaking things apart until procrastination would seem silly. If a performance evaluation session is uncomfortable, start by reviewing the file, then scheduling the meeting, then "scripting" your opening comments.

Remove (or have someone remove) what I call the "procrastination alleys." These are the escape routes you currently use. Don't try to work on something with your guitar sitting in the corner. Turn off your computer screen and smart phone. Don't listen to music. Move to a conference room without windows and get out of your office.

Procrastination is both a manifestation of fear and fear-induced. It is a double-edged sword and it's critical to blunt it. We mistake it for the natural outcome of the intellectually curious, or assign it (as we do too many faults today) to Attention Deficit Disorder, or we call it "human nature." But it is far more insidious when it's not faced candidly.

Procrastination is drenched in fear and thrives in fear. We need to overcome that to be fearless leaders. It is highly visible, can readily influence others, and often results in still other dysfunctional behaviors which we'll talk about next.

Passive-Aggressive Behaviors

Passive-aggressive behavior is indirect resistance to others' needs and suggestions (and even observations), avoiding direct confrontation through subtle sarcasm and even procrastination.

Passive-aggressive people might repeatedly make excuses as to why things aren't done. They will repeatedly claim nothing is personal and that they are quite all right even when it's apparent they're angry. These are people who do not allow emotional vulnerability, and are often out to undermine you.

It is often intimidating to try to deal with them.

Case Study

I had a manager, Gary, who would swear to me every month that his yearly goal would be made even though he was behind. He showed me forecasts and projections that placed the preponderance of the year in the fourth quarter.

In November, when it was clear he would not make his goals, he told me at a public meeting that the goals were never realistic and that he had never really committed to them.

I fired him the next day.

As opposed to procrastination based in the fear of being critiqued for the final product, these personalities procrastinate to deliberately cause harm to others as a "punishment," to assuage their own anger.

The causes of passive-aggressive behavior vary, but they are primarily grounded in:

- Alienation: The individual feels left out or excluded where overt displays of anger are not socially acceptable so covert mechanisms are used.
- Nurturing: This occurs in households where emotions are kept tightly in check and where manifestations of feelings are discouraged or even punished. Therefore, anger and frustration must find other, more passive, outlets.
- Sloth: It takes work and discipline to maturely express emotions such as anger, disappointment, frustration, and guilt. Bracing yourself against resistance can be uncomfortable and painful. It's easier not to confront, therefore, but to undermine.

Fear Factor

Passive-aggressive behaviors tend to bring out the worst traits in leaders because they are hard to confront, seem supportive at least superficially, and strike when you least expect it. You have to confront them in the moment.

Since many leaders can become fearful about dealing with such people, it's important to overcome that fear with some effective tactics:

1. Recognize it for what it is. Damning with faint praise, undermining comments, procrastination, failure to respond, and minimal communications are all indicators.

2. Keep your own anger in check once you recognize the symptoms. Confront the other person with observed behavior, evidence of actions or inactions, and verbatim quotes. Don't be afraid to say, "Why would you say something so obviously harmful?"

Case Study

One of the most chronic, deeply disturbed passive-aggressive people I've ever met was a mother of one of our children's friends in school. I'll call her "Molly." When our daughter was accepted into the Newhouse School at Syracuse University, arguably the best broadcast journalism school in the country, Molly commented to my wife in front of others, "Congratulations. I assume that was her backup school?" The personality disorder is that bad!

3. Usually, you'll receive denial and more passive-aggressive behavior. ("I'm just trying to comply with your own examples of providing feedback honestly.") Continue to confront. When it's realized that the behavior isn't having its intended (detrimental) effect, most people will back off.

Are you passive-aggressive at times?

Fearless leadership is about acknowledging emotions, confronting behavior, and taking the high road. You're not being fearless if you engage in this very destructive, insidious behavior yourself.

Here's a quick test:

• Do you give people the "silent treatment" when you are upset with or angry at them? (This is often done in poor marriages.) Do you clam-up instead of speak up?

- Do you subvert otherwise meaningful and sophisticated conversation with sarcasm and derail the discussion? Do you make fun of people in front of others? ("Looks like you have a speech impediment there!")
- Do you become depressed and withdraw when you are unhappy with someone rather than confront them with honest conversation?
- Do you avoid even seeing people? Are you hard to make an appointment with unless the other person is a close friend or colleague?
- Do you procrastinate in an attempt to punish someone else and undermine their efforts?

If even two of these conditions apply to you:

Improve your recognition of your own actions and behaviors. Recognize why you are upset and what your options are to maturely and forcefully deal with your frustrations.

Understand exactly what your emotions are and what they're causing. Don't focus on what you *think*, but rather on what you *feel*. Learn how to express and act on your feelings in a dignified manner. You may need coaching or even therapy to accomplish this.

Don't expect to change overnight. Passive-aggressive behavior is generally of long-standing and highly reinforced by your own mindset. Allow yourself time and don't beat yourself up for not immediately transforming yourself.

Can't-Pull-The-Trigger Syndrome

One of the manifestations of fear is the refusal or inability to act in the moment, to act when the potential for positive results is highest. I call this a failure to "pull the trigger." This is, of course, metaphorical, and no one can die making leadership decisions, even wrong ones.

I want to make it clear that I'm a big fan of due diligence for appropriate decisions and initiatives. You shouldn't be hiring an advertising agency, or buying an off-shore facility, or changing your pension fund investments, or investing in property without a boatload of due diligence. That's when all those conservative lawyers finally earn their pay.

Even when hiring for key positions or promoting into them, it's wise and savvy to take your time and ensure you're making the best possible choice with the maximum information. It's easy to hire a lousy person but very difficult to get rid of a lousy person. It's very much like quicksand: The more you struggle, the faster you sink.

Thus, having apparently tried to dismantle much of my point (!), I'm going to explain why fearless leadership requires a hair trigger and a willingness to shoot. We are often faced with surprise, abrupt, and high potential choices. We can change our plans and attend a developmental experience we just learned about that begins next week. We can invest in a new fund with limited openings that we're hoping doesn't replicate Bernie Madoff. We can buy that new car that the dealer had ordered for someone who reneged on it. We can fire a non-performing executive who seems momentarily susceptible to a good severance offer.

But when we equivocate, the car is sold, the development is bypassed, the fund closes for new investment, the executive decides to stay on and play hardball, threatening a lawsuit or board appeal. We have moved from the offensive to the defensive.

Defenses don't win games. You have to pull the trigger.

We fear pulling that trigger because:

- We're urged to be cautious by everyone from our parents to our spouses, from our attorneys to our mentors.
- We feel we can't "undo" any harm done, can't "un-ring" the bell.
- We believe there is "always time" to come back and get to it, despite warnings that the opportunity won't last.
- We fail to do a proper risk evaluation *and consistently overrate the risk without really thinking about it carefully.*
- We take comfort in bringing in others, getting consensus, and finding support—just in case we're making the biggest mistake of our lives.

When my dogs spy an open gate on our property, they run through it. They don't stop to do an "opportunity analysis" or bring in other dogs to evaluate the possibilities. They simply charge through the damn gate, tongues flapping and tails wagging. Dogs are always ready to pull the trigger.

Fear Factor

We equate cautious movement with wisdom and prudence. Jack Welch, Steve Jobs, Bill Gates, Warren Buffett, Ronald Reagan, Oprah Winfrey, Tiger Woods, Steven Spielberg, Barack Obama—they had no trouble pulling the trigger, and they don't exactly constitute a pantheon of failure.

What's the difference between assertive action and precipitous action for a leader? What are lines of demarcation among cautious, fearless, and foolhardy?

If you're *overly cautious* you:

- Seek consensus on all occasions
- Measure three times and then maybe not cut at all
- Look for precedent and guarantees of success
- Refuse to consider ameliorating risk or preventing it
- "Think on it" and, yes, procrastinate
- Use logic exclusively and never your emotions ("gut")

If you're *foolhardy* you:

- Decide without considering options or alternatives
- Ignore risk entirely
- Never consider impact on others
- Never consult a coach or expert
- Commit to action without proper resources or support
- Use emotion exclusively and never your logic ("brain")

If you are *effectively assertive* you:

- Quickly evaluate risk and both preventive and contingent actions
- Consider options and choose among or combine them
- Rapidly consult a coach or trusted advisor
- Ensure the decision will gain commitment and support
- Are comfortable setting precedent, breaking new ground
- Effectively combine logic and emotions

Here's a quick way to look at risk:

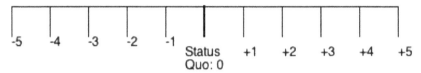

-5   -4   -3   -2   -1   Status   +1   +2   +3   +4   +5
                            Quo: 0

Question: What is the best and worst that might result?

+5= Paradigm-beaking improvement, industry leader.
+4= Dramatic improvement, major publicity.
+3= Strong benefits, organization-wide.
+2= Minor benefits, localized.
+1= Very minor improvement, barely noticed.

-1= Very minor setback, barely noticed.
-2= Minor setback, controlled locally.
-3= Public setback, requires damage control.
-4= Major defeat, financial damages, recovery time needed.
-5= Devastating losses.

Risk evaluation.

In making decisions, you always want a potential positive result from the status quo that's greater than the possible negative result. The key is to use actions that prevent the negative outcome from occurring *and* ameliorating actions which mitigate the effects should they occur anyway. (If the "no smoking" sign didn't prevent a fire caused by careless smoking, then the sprinkler system will douse it).

Fearless leaders aren't fools. They are simply people who know best how to evaluate risk and effectively control it, thereby freeing themselves to be bold and to pull the trigger faster and more often than others.

Refusal to Leave the Nest

I've coined a phrase, "nesting syndrome," which is meant to depict our conscious or unconscious refusal to leave comfortable circumstances we've created for ourselves (the antithesis of "fearless"). We stop creating challenges and resist challenges from others. We feel as if we've "made it" and earned our position, so why rock this boat? (I think this is especially prevalent at senior leadership positions in professional service firms.)

Here are some manifestations and traits. Do any of these apply to you?

1. The unconscious competency trap: We perform on autopilot and therefore experience insufficient self-awareness, become oblivious to opportunities around us, and simply keep the nest neat.
2. The refusal to shake things up: We adopt the tired adage, "If it ain't broke, don't fix it," which enables us to resist extra work. Our mantra should be, "If it ain't broke, improve it."
3. Failure to create new value for customers: We assume that everyone is happy, neglect to innovate, and wind up like Sears instead of Amazon.
4. Failure to exploit referral business: We believe our current customer picture is THE picture, believing it to be a movie continuing into tomorrow instead of merely a snapshot of today.
5. "King of the Hill" syndrome: We're seldom challenged because of our hierarchical position, our levels of "filters," a retinue of "yes-people," and our repute. But when we're not challenged we're not growing. Jack Welch went from "Neutron Jack" who only left the buildings standing to someone highly concerned about GE's human assets. I used to watch him in "the pit" in Crotonville, New York (GE's training

center), handling questions from anyone who cared to hurl one down on him.

Fear Factor

Nests disintegrate in stormy weather, and sometimes the very branches in which they're lodged are sawed off.

6. Problem solving instead of innovation: Fixing things provides immediate gratification and you know if something once worked it can be made to work again. But that merely restores past levels of performance. Conformist innovation produced Uber, a more sophisticated taxi company concept. But non-conformist innovation produced Amazon, an entirely unique entity. (Ask yourself why Sears, a pioneer in catalogs, use of railroads, and retail stores didn't morph into Amazon. The answer is consistently lousy, fearful leadership.)
7. Avoidance of sharp turns: Fearless leadership means that you're willing to depart from the current road (the nest) and blaze new trails. When I worked with Calgon they were number three in the water treatment business and were miles behind the two leaders. Calgon

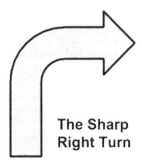

**The Sharp
Right Turn**

Figure 3.1   *The sharp right turn.*

changed its identity into "effluent management" and immediately became the number one firm in that field (Figure 3.1).

8. Refusal to fire people: Nowhere is fearless leadership more important than in recognizing and acting on those who no longer are contributing to the business. Too many leaders see themselves running an employment agency. Keeping these people only helps to feather and maintain the existing nest. If the leader doesn't fire them, they'll never go. I remember walking through a division of a Fortune 10 client with the general manager. I asked how things were. "Not so good since Joe retired," said the GM. "But Joe's sitting right over there!" I observed, to which the GM replied, "Oh, I didn't say he left, I just said he retired."

9. Chasing money as a high priority: If the metric in use is to maximize short-term profits, then that's what will be sought and rewarded. That's what we've seen at Volkswagen, Wells Fargo, Enron, and other disasters in the business world. Leadership is about creating value for customers and investors. Profits improve value, but so do ethical conduct, community citizenship, revenue growth, retention of talent, and investments in R&D and product commercialization.

10. Fear of failure and refusal to experiment: Playing it safe leads, literally, nowhere. We talk a great deal about volatility and disruption today, but the key behavior for fearless leaders *is to create the disruption themselves internally.* Abandon a line of business, form a new alliance, identify a new, ideal customer cohort. If you're not failing in this world, you're just not trying hard enough.

How many of these are you "guilty" of perpetuating? Some people are so successful at feathering their nests that they forget how to fly altogether. So when a storm comes along and upends the nest, everything falls apart and hits the ground.

When I was growing up, the major industries were steel, rubber, textile, and automotive. Not so much today. International Business Machine was present, however, and despite the name, they didn't consider themselves to be in the business machine business or the punch card business. They considered themselves in the information transfer business. Today, most of their profit comes from consulting services.

Lou Gerstner, brought in from outside the notoriously incestuous IBM culture, transformed the organization. That was a fearless decision by the board, and he exemplified fearless leadership. Who would ever think that the vaunted GE would hit the skids as it did in 2018 and beyond, after Jack Welch retired?

You can be fearful or fearless. Not much of a choice.

CHAPTER 4

Erasing Past Fears

We often fear things despite massive evidence to the contrary that we have nothing to fear. Fear is visceral, so we seldom ask why *we're afraid. The answer to that question is revelatory.*

When our kids were young we would vacation on the Jersey shore. There was a long boardwalk in Wildwood, New Jersey, that featured a "fun house." You boarded a car on rails which took you through the amusement in the dark.

My son refused to take the ride. "Don't be afraid of the dark," I pontificated.

"I'm not afraid of the dark," he assured me.

"Then why won't you take the ride?" I pressed.

"Because I'm afraid of what might be in the dark."

The Evidentiary Test

Despite all evidence to the contrary, we tend to believe everything from myths, to rumors, to stark falsehoods. "Who are you going to believe?" we're often asked. "Me or your lying eyes?!"

Thus, on the fringes, people swear to sasquatch, yeti, UFOs, ghosts, and levitation. But well within the fringes, well within the "norms," people believe they're incompetent even though they've performed wonderfully in the past, that they're imposters, even though clients keep rehiring them or buying from them, and frauds, even though people swear by their results.

Despite all evidence to the contrary, we believe the worst and fear the worst. Empirical evidence be damned, I can't believe my lying eyes.

Our fears from the past cast a giant shadow on our current reality. We need to get rid of that shadow because we need light for our future.

Case Study

My coaching client created insightful, action-oriented reports for clients on reducing dangerous conditions in their operations. He was consistently making over a half-million dollars a year, and clients were thrilled with his work.

However, each new project found him at the deadline for the report, at midnight the prior evening, desperately toiling to complete the latest analysis, usually in its fourth draft. He created such onerous work for himself because he was certain the report would not be good and would disappoint the client, so nothing he produced was good enough. He would finally turn in the last iteration because he was out of time.

And the client always loved it.

But despite this overwhelming evidence to the contrary, he persisted in his laborious approaches, not because he thought they worked, but because he was afraid not to.

Often, conditions change in our lives and work. I was a starting basketball player in high school but didn't even think about trying out for my college team because that was an entirely different level of competition. Sometimes people change, including ourselves. We develop new skills or forget how to do something. While you don't forget (normally) how to ride a bike, you can forget how to make a necktie knot or prepare a certain food. That's because the bike is a muscle skill but the others are cognitive.

Older people may forget names and dates, but if they're physically fit, they don't forget how to ride a bike.

The evidentiary test calls for us to ask two questions to overcome fears:

1. Have I ever done this successfully or come close?
2. Has anyone ever done this successfully who is a reasonable model for me to emulate?

I might not emulate Tom Brady at quarterback, but if my friend, with similar physical abilities, played the position, why couldn't I if I were so inclined? Fearing failure or others' critique should never be a factor.

Fear Factor

We tend to ignore empirical evidence of our success and create myths about our probable failures.

The primary requirement to eradicate past fears that haunt us today is to get rid of the old baggage. But that's not as simple as it sounds, *because we do need baggage and can't get along without it.*

The old inappropriate baggage is tough to jettison because:

- It was accurate at one time. I *was* unprepared, I *did* try to get out of responsibilities.
- The source was profound. Your parents were respected in the community, paid for your schooling, acted responsibly. What they told you was unequivocally true.
- The baggage is comfortable. You know your supposed weaknesses and strengths, and it provides security.

The problem here is that others packed that baggage. You have to get rid of it and pack new baggage.

Some things you were told were and are false: Don't go swimming for exactly one hour after you've eaten. Don't run with a stick or you'll poke your eye out.*

Some things were isolated and minor, but built into universals and therefore major. You missed a kick in soccer and you're told you're a lousy athlete when, in fact, you missed just one kick. You received a poor mark in a test, and you're told you're a lousy student. (How many times did you get a good mark and were told you're a "scholar"? Or were you told you were simply "lucky" that time?)

Some things were simply mean and undermining. Siblings are particularly good at this kind of damage, and so are parents for whom you can't "win sufficiently." ("Your grades are the best in your class, but still below what your older sister's were.") We see the same in business today: "You had a great year, but it wasn't as good as the record Bob set five years ago."

Too often we also use the wrong metrics. We use other people's metrics. It's common for a professional speaker to point to evaluations sheets that give her a 9.8 out of 10, or seek standing ovations after the session. But if you're called upon to provoke an audience and make the members uncomfortable—that's why the client is paying you—those metrics don't apply. Why apply them? If I want to enjoy myself on the ski slopes, I really don't care that you can zoom down black diamond hills all day, I'm happy on the intermediate slopes. *Trying to prove myself by your performance won't make me happy and might get me killed.*

To begin overcoming past fears we have to accept empirical evidence—what I'm calling "the evidentiary test"—to assess whether our fears are well-founded or simply ridiculous, and they're usually the latter.

Comedian Jerry Seinfeld pointed out once that surveys showed that the fear of public speaking exceeded the fear of death for most people. "That means," he observed, "that the person delivering the eulogy is in worse shape than the person in the coffin."

---

* I can't count how many times my friends and I looked closely at the time because it was only 54 minutes after lunch and if we went into the water then we'd get cramps and drown. But we did run with sharp sticks!

That sounds utterly preposterous until you consider why people profess to a fear of merely speaking in public. There is no sound reason for it, but there is a notorious reason: ego protection. But you can't allow your ego to dictate your actions today based on past baggage. Let's examine how to transition.

Transitioning to Current Reality

The mere sighting of certain creatures (real or imagined) throughout history has been cause for fear: snakes (even harmless ones), spiders, bees, sharks, the Medusa, black cats. It's generally believed that the current practice of a handshake upon meeting someone stems from an ancient practice of disclosing an empty hand to prove there was no weapon in it, thus lowering the fear of a stranger.

Similarly, many situations and circumstances viscerally create fear: heights, plane rides, public speaking, tests and exams, medical procedures and injections.

Are our experiences of the past—both our species' past and our personal past—unduly causing us fear in our daily lives?

Oh, yeah!

Few people have ever been bitten by a snake, most of which will flee from humans. Few people have been bitten by spiders, and the vast majority of such bites are harmless. The odds of being in a plane crash in the US are about one in eleven million[*] compared to the lifetime chances of dying from unintentional poisoning of all kinds which are one in 70, compared with 1 in 583 in a car accident and 1 in 114,195 for fatal injuries caused by lightning.[†]

Yet people readily drive every day, which is far more hazardous than flying.

---

[*] https://www.elitedaily.com/news/world/people-terrified-plane-crashes-even-though-rare/977885

[†] https://www.cars.com/articles/are-the-odds-ever-in-your-favor-car-crashes-versus-other-fatalities-1420682154567/

Case Study

I encounter a great many coaching clients who ask me about rare and
even bizarre client situations, and what they should do about them.
One example is what I call "the gun in the drawer question."

A client asks me what to do if the client across the desk keeps opening and closing a desk drawer, and then the coach looks in there and
sees a gun.

"Has that ever happened to you?" I ask.

"Well, no," my client inevitably replies.

There are many people who *create* fearful circumstances that don't
actually exist and have a ridiculously low probability of occurring.
That is, they don't reflect current reality at all.

Police officers put their lives on the line for us daily. Imagine if they
were fearful of what might happen to the point of ineffectiveness? But it's a
sought-after job performed overwhelmingly well by men and women inter-
ested in the public's well-being and protection. How can these people be so
sanguine?

According to Pew Research[*] only 27 percent of police officers have ever
fired their gun outside of the practice range while on duty. The New York
City police force alone has close to 40,000 full-time officers, larger than
many countries' armies. Despite the headlines, the job isn't all that dangerous; in fact, it doesn't make the top ten most dangerous jobs in the US
according to *Time*.[†] (For the record, the top ten are logging workers, fish-
ing workers, aircraft pilots, roofers, trash collectors, iron and steel workers,
truck drivers, farmers and ranchers, front line supervisors in construction,
and ground maintenance workers—in terms of fatal injuries per 100,000
workers. Note that firefighters are not on the list, either.)

---

[*] http://www.pewresearch.org/fact-tank/2017/02/08/a-closer-look-at-police-officers-who-have-
fired-their-weapon-on-duty/

[†] http://time.com/5074471/most-dangerous-jobs/

When a cat jumps on a hot stove, it will in the future refrain from jumping on a cold one as well. When a salesperson endures a bad situation from a certain type of buyer (e.g., older, younger, large office, financial background, and so forth), that experience will tend to create fear in the next situation that resembles it, despite the fact that there are really vastly different people involved. One suddenly vicious dog can make us paranoid about all strange dogs.

But those aren't rational reactions.

Our parents have warned us about certain dangers (running with a sharp stick), as have our doctors (being overweight is dangerous), as have our siblings (you'll probably break your leg like I did when you try to ski), as have our employers (never argue with a customer), as have our experiences (don't pet dogs). Some of these are valid, some are projection,* some are exaggerations, and some are simply wrong.

Are you capable of discerning which is which?

Well, I'm here to help you do that.

Fear Factor

Most things that we were legitimately *afraid of no longer are legitimate. The high school bully, the animal howling in the woods, the horrible teacher who humiliated us—they are gone, just like your training wheels and your dental retainer. Get in touch with today's reality.*

Here's how you can make the transition to today's reality and becoming more fearless:

1. Identify the things that you should legitimately fear but are out of your control to prevent. This would include war, hurricanes, earthquakes,

---

* The assignment of a flaw of the person advising to the person being advised. You won't be able to play the piano because I couldn't learn it, and if you did learn it that might mean I'm somehow inferior to you.

and loss of loved ones. But understand that you can take *contingent actions* in many of these cases. You can plan to evacuate your premises, have liquid savings available, and spend as much time as you can with your loved ones at the moment.

2. Be aware that many things can be reduced in likelihood or actually prevented. Even some dread diseases, such as cancer, can be reduced by lifestyle choices. Where you choose to live can reduce the probability of natural disasters. I have four million air miles, but wouldn't choose today to travel on a notoriously poorly maintained plane run by an airline with a poor safety record.

3. Create control over those issues and events where you can exert influence, especially preventive action. Prepare well for a speech and practice it with a coach. Go to a zoo or nature preserve and learn about snakes, which of them are harmful and which are not, and what to do when you encounter one. Don't drink and drive, and don't drive on those occasions (e.g., New Year's Eve) when you know many other people will be drinking and driving.

Transitioning to your current reality means giving up—throwing off the train along with old baggage—those fears that were always illegitimate (spiders) and those that were once legitimate and no longer apply (vaccine injections and blood tests).

You have to isolate yourself to a degree and ask, "Who am I today, what are my relationships, what is my career, and what are my plans?" You'll find that while most courses of action include risk, those risks are never fatal and seldom issues that can't be prevented or ameliorated.

Your default behavior can't be fear and can't be flight. *There is no gun in the drawer.*

Asking "Why?"

The quickest way to eliminate the effects of past fears on your life today is to ask the simple question, "Why?" Then use indisputable facts to overcome the fear.

"I'm afraid to fly. Why? Because I might die."
Facts:

- No one has been killed in a US commercial airline crash in 10 years, which is safer than driving or making household repairs. Do you drive and make household repairs?
- Over four billion people fly every year, many of whom have less sophistication and intelligence than you do!
- You can obtain counseling or coaching and even take sedatives with medical advice.

"I'm afraid of speaking before a group. Why? Because they will determine that I'm not good at what I do and I'll make a fool of myself."
Facts:

- Others in your company with less talent than you do this regularly.
- Your boss made a bad error in a talk last month and everyone kidded about it and he joked about it.
- You have the option to be coached on public speaking.
- The last time you spoke, several people said they learned a great deal.

"I'm afraid to confront the boss even though what she's requesting is unreasonable and won't be done on time. Why? Because this project is her top priority and she won't want to hear that it's unworkable in present form."
Facts:

- The last time your colleagues gave her feedback she was attentive and altered her plans.
- You have a good relationship and she has given you strong evaluations.
- She is pleasant and most approachable at the beginning of the day.

"I'm afraid of launching a solo career, working for myself. Why? Because my spouse is very dubious about it and I don't know that I can generate sufficient income for our current expenses on my own."

Facts:

- You have enough money in the bank and among your investments for at least nine months of expenses and the experts recommend that you need six.
- Your spouse's father failed at his own business, and you have to differentiate between his unreasonable investment in an untried product and your investment in what you've been doing all along for someone else.
- You have access to a coach who has helped other people launch businesses that have become highly successful within six months.
- You could access your retirement funds if absolutely necessary.

We tend to accept fears consciously or unconsciously without critical evaluation of their causes. Here are some important relationships:

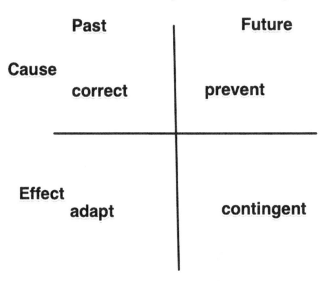

Past and future relationships.

As you can see in the illustration, we can remove past issues by eliminating the cause of the fear. However, too often we merely adapt to the manifestations of the fear. So we avoid heights, or decline to speak, or fail to confront, or keep our mouths shut. We become so adept at adapting that it becomes our default position *and we give it no more conscious thought.*

In the future, we can plan to prevent the fear altogether, or ameliorate whatever frightening effects we contemplate. (Take a "fear of flying" workshop but also have medication to take on the plane if needed.)

Fear Factor

We can become so unconsciously adept at dealing with our limitations caused by fears that we never actively try to eliminate their causes. This is a self-deceptive, protective measure which must be raised to the surface and overcome.

Asking "Why?" always brings us to the *cause* if we're honest in our replies. "Why am I afraid to cite a six-figure proposal to a prospect?" If the answer is "I'm not worth that much," or "The client would never have that kind of budget," or "It's inappropriate to ask that much," you're simply not dealing with the real cause (the real "why").

Why are you really afraid? Because you're feeling like an imposter who doesn't deserve that kind of money. You father always told you that you wouldn't amount to anything, or your siblings told you that consulting wasn't a real profession, or your colleagues told you that the only way to charge is by the hour. Once you dismiss your father as callow, and your siblings as jealous, and your colleagues as dinosaurs, you can charge whatever you want because the causes of your fear have been eradicated or proved untrue.

Case Study

My client told me that he broke out into such an anxious state that he could only wear blue suits and dark shirts so the perspiration wouldn't show when he spoke. I asked if this happened every time.

"About a quarter of the time it does not, and I walk on stage without any nerves and perfectly dry," he said.

I asked him "Why?" for that 25 percent of the time, what was distinctive, and found out that he was engaged with people right up to being introduced. He didn't have time to think about his nerves or the audience.

I told him to deliberately engage people every time in the future, or listen to music, or watch something on his iPad, right up to the introduction. He never had an anxious moment again prior to his speaking.

We can ask "Why?" for others.

Asking "Why?" is, in fact, finding *cause*. Once you know the cause of your fears you can take effective action to reduce their probability of occurring (visit a doctor or dentist for preventive checkups) and/or reduce their severity (buy insurance, create a "nest egg") as seen in the above illustration.

Many people have a visceral reaction to a fear by fleeing from it or being paralyzed by fright. Fighting the fear—often called "facing the fear"—requires that you overcome the default, visceral reaction by creating a different response: Finding out *why* you are reacting the way you are.

I mentioned earlier that we couldn't be certain there was never a monster under the bed. But we might've looked on any given night and not found one. Thus it does mean that particular night we were assured there was none and we could get a good sleep. *Soon, that became our norm.*

The Curse of Rumination

To "ruminate" is to think deeply about something—*often way too deeply*. We ruminate to delay, to protect, to ensure, to guarantee. In other words, we ruminate to satisfy our fears about actually taking action.

And a "ruminant," of course, is an animal that repeatedly chews its cud over, and over, and over. And over.

Pessimism thrives on its reciprocity with fear, while optimism is an anti-dote to fear. Whether one is resilient or ruminant is determined by those opposing mindsets, as you can see in Figure 4.1.

If something adverse has occurred in the past and we are naturally pessimistic, we ruminate about it. We tend to wonder whether it can happen again, if we should have been able to avoid it, if we've been unlucky, or if we've been clueless.

We dwell on past fears instead of erasing them.

When we're optimistic, we learn from the experience. We realize that a poor hour doesn't make a poor day, and a poor day doesn't make a poor life. A poor conversation doesn't poison an entire relationship. A poor decision doesn't doom us. We are resilient.

When we look to the future as a pessimist, we dread. Our fears overwhelm us about the unknown, and we can't rationally overcome them because we feel a loss of influence and control. We experience a Calvinistic pre-determination that external forces will control us. But when we look ahead optimistically, we see opportunity, and the ability to control, influence, and mold our futures. There are very few fears which can't be managed successfully.

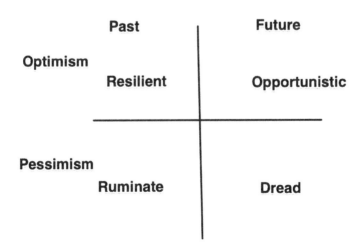

Figure 4.1 *Pessimism and optimism.*

These four conditions: resilience and opportunism, and rumination and dread, are stark opposites. To erase our past fears (and alleviate our future ones) we need to firmly embed ourselves in an optimistic world view.

Fear Factor

Optimism and pessimism are choices. They are not in our DNA nor in our surroundings. We decide to be positive or negative, and that choice determines whether our fears remain with us and create deeper roots, or are exercised and tossed off the train with the rest of the inappropriate baggage.

These fears from the past which remain with us today are often caused by factors associated with the fear. For example, a snake isn't feared so much as its attributes (real or imagined) in terms of speed, stealth, fangs, and slime. Similarly, public speaking has been fearful because of its attributes of being on a stage with a light on you, being judged by others, and making mistakes without any place to hide. (Has anyone ever gone through life *without* the nightmare of suddenly being naked in a public place?)

A *schema* is a representation of these attributes to form cognitive reactions to a perceived threat, triggering emotional responses of fear. We postulate harm, lack of control, ugliness, humiliation. In reality, of course, the snake just wants to go on its way hunting for a rodent and the audience really wants you to succeed.*

Fear is a negative emotional state triggered by some stimulus (some schema) like the snake or the speech. The threat isn't really present (the snake isn't attacking and the audience isn't heckling) but is perceived and even anticipated. The line between mere anxiety (as in passing a test) and true fear isn't all that thick. After any trauma, for example (a fire, a plane

---

* When I coach speakers I have to convince them that only sociopaths would desire going home to brag that they sat through a horrible hour's speech and enjoyed watching a speaker go down in flames. Healthy people want a successful experience.

crash, an illness), we tend to be overly concerned, more than just anxious, and probably fearful of a repeat. Someone I know who was in an auto accident while riding in a taxi today continually gives taxis and Uber drivers warnings from the back seat on every trip. The scientific basis for this is our old friend the amygdala, which connects two events to create a "memory." When the otherwise neutral act occurs—the snake's evidence in the grass, the request to speak—the amygdala, unfortunately, stimulates you like the real danger would have. *Thus, we're responding to danger unconsciously and must raise it to conscious level in order to deal with it and eradicate it.*

True fear, the need to flee legitimate danger, is quite common in virtually all organisms. But dread about what may be coming and the operation of our schema are uniquely human. *We can, unfortunately, project our fears and anxieties into the future with a rare impact and meticulousness.*

Trusting your judgment is the escape hatch, not trying to prevent yourself from projecting into the future, which is impossible. But judgment is also a largely human trait (at least to its full potential), and its role can be seen in Figure 4.2.

The box lists what I call the "hyper-traits" of judgment. You can develop these factors, thus you can always improve your judgment. When things go well and you make intelligent decisions, your successes reinforce your trust in your judgment and further refine the hyper-traits. When things go

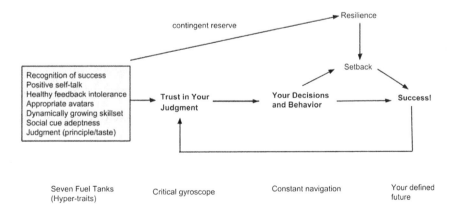

Figure 4.2   *The key role of judgment.*

wrong—as they do for all of us—the hyper-traits also provide the resilience we discussed above to move us back from a position of setback to a position of success.

Case Study

I was working with the top team of a Fortune 25 company, everyone in the room making high six figures or more, and every one of them afraid to approach the CEO with a plan for expansion they were positive he'd feel was insufficiently aggressive. I was bewildered, because I had coached the CEO on several occasions, and we had both survived and prospered from differences of opinion on some key issues.

I found that the group was afraid of the meeting, not of the content. Their visceral (amygdalan) and incorrect reaction (schema) was that the CEO would immediately attack any position not consistent with his own time frames. I convinced them that what he expected was honesty and something he could take to the board and say his entire team was behind. We role-played a half-dozen different openings, chose a spokesperson, and had a great meeting that afternoon.

The group came to realize they were not seeing and would not see a snake, and the audience wanted them to succeed.

Summary

You can't "deal with" or "manage" past fears. They form too much of the schema that influence your present and future. You have to eradicate them. That's best done by asking yourself why you still possess them, what evidence contradicts them, applying your contemporary reality, and avoiding rumination about the past.

These are learnable and evergreen skills. But you have to be willing to implant them and nurture them. You can't be afraid of what might be in the dark.

CHAPTER 5

Preventing Future Fears

.

The worst kind of fear is over those issues for which you lack all control. This is useless fear, but nonetheless paralyzing. Fear is overcome by failing and rebounding, not by trying never to fail.

Avoiding "Dread"

"Dread" means a fear of and apprehension about the future. It's often used colloquially—"I dread going to dinner with those people"—and often seriously—"I am dreading the impact of the quarterly results"—and is also often unspoken altogether.

That is, dread is also a "mood," a feeling of imminent danger and adverse consequence. There is pervasive dread when a soldier is missing in action, or someone is kidnapped, or the IRS is auditing the books. That dread creates its own kind of fear, because we are "caught in the headlights" and unable to make a decision that, for all we know, might make things worse. Of course, being frozen in place is also usually a bad outcome.

In leadership, dread undermines rational thinking and can create a near-panic situation. If your pet is undergoing surgery at the vet, or your child is flunking out of college, or your spouse's family is moving in, you want a quick, positive resolution which is probably impossible to obtain.

The same occurs when your largest customer leaves you an ambiguous message about "discussing the future," in which case you're very eager to talk, although they mentioned next week, and you're simultaneously happy that you have a week to prepare, but also not happy about being granted a full week to dread a worst case outcome! Dread moves all your emotional gauges over the "red line," and your decisions will therefore often be short-term, or overly conciliatory, or simply wrong.

Most of us, most of the time, when faced with unavoidable suffering, we'll try to get it over with. It's as simple as that. Get the shot from the doctor, face the angry client, fire your cousin despite the family's outrage. People—think about your own past reactions—tend to accelerate the confrontation of the dread and even accept greater pain *in order to get it over with*. "Let's go in and get this over with" has prefaced many a board presentation or evaluation session.

My contention here is that accepting short-term pain is far superior than enduring long-term dread. This is another version of the "threshold phenomenon" we discussed earlier.

Fear Factor

People can fall into a "dread state" without even realizing it, and if it's sustained or frequent, will consider it "normal."

Thus, once an action is determined to be required, people opt to endure the pain and perform what's necessary. This ends the "dread" of worrying about doing it.

Merely expecting the awful can itself be awful. That applies to a colonoscopy, a huge roller coaster ride, or even a first date. It certainly applies to dealing with difficult colleagues and subordinates at work.

Therefore, we need *distractions* to refocus us away from the dreadful anticipation.

Just as studying something affects what you're studying (Heisenberg Principle), anticipating an emotional event (dread) *is itself an emotional event*, which triggers all kinds of emotional and psychological (and even physical) reactions. Hence, *distracting* oneself from the prefatory dread is critically important.

We all seek to avoid anxiety if we're mentally healthy. We'd rather deal with the unpleasant in an active manner than contemplate and await the unpleasant in a passive manner.

If the batter "dreads" the star pitcher's fastball, he'll never hit it. If the prima ballerina dreads the review of the theater critic in the audience, she'll probably not dance well. If you, as a leader or entrepreneur, dread the next client meeting, it probably won't go well. *And if we dread failure, we're in the wrong line of work, because failure is inevitable and is a learning experience.*

The pursuit of perfection undermines excellence and causes unending dread!

The royal road here is clear:

- Recognize and identify if you're in a "dread" state situationally or as a matter of course. This will be symbolized by feelings of anxiety of approaching pain and a lack of positive action.
- Accept the pain short term and even accelerate it. Have the band-aid torn off the scab!
- Develop actions that deal with worst-case events and put them in place, but do not default to the worst-case event before you reach the outcome of your meeting or event or confrontation or experience.
- Create distractions that effectively prevent you from focusing on the issue. Play with the dog, go to an event, interact with friends, get out of the office.

Dread is actually an emotion in response to or anticipation of other emotions. Deal with what's actually causing the anxiety, don't create additional anxiety.

Many people dread divorce and its aftermath so they live in the pain of a poor relationship for the rest of their lives. But some are willing to accept the immediate pain of divorce to save the rest of their lives, overcoming their dread and eventually creating happiness. ***I've found among my coaching clients that this is the key determinant as to whether irreconcilable differences are dealt with in the present or are allowed to ruin the future.***

Establishing Resilience

Resilience is the ability to recover quickly, to "spring back" from an upset, defeat, setback, or other unanticipated obstacle. Resilience counteracts fear. If you have history of and/or confidence in your resilience you don't fear (dread) defeat and disappointment to any great degree.

Consequently, resilience is one of the greatest emotional tools to combat fear.

I've studied resilience quite closely in my coaching work and co-authored *The Resilience Advantage* with Dr. Richard Citrin.* I have found that *resilience can be developed methodically although some people possess it inherently.* Even for the latter, it's important to understand the components since that "conscious competency" makes it replicable.

To actively develop resilience, consider the following deliberate actions until they become your default behaviors:

- Recognition of success: This is the willingness to identify past successes, retain their impact, and duplicate their causes.

---

* Business Expert Press, 2018.

- Positive self-talk: The habit of looking at "challenges" and not "problems" and asking how to do something and not resolving that you can't do it.*
- Healthy feedback intolerance: Most *unsolicited* feedback is for the benefit and ego of the sender, not the recipient. We need to disregard all of it if we're not to become ping pong balls.
- Appropriate avatars: Whom do we really respect and admire who can provide us with a sample of how we should act and behave under a variety of situations. How can we become both gracious winners and gracious losers at times?
- Dynamically growing skillset: As we improve and grow, we should continue to raise our own "bar" and metrics. *This is the key to becoming better and not merely older.*
- Social cue adeptness: We need to be aware of our environment, our impact on others, and appropriate behavior for the circumstances. Many of us have heard from a spouse or partner, "You're not at work now, change your tone!"
- Judgment (principles and taste): Thomas Jefferson said, "In matters of taste, swim with the tide, in matters of principle stand like a rock." We need to modulate our reactions based on the import and gravity (or lack thereof) of our situation.

These traits allow us to have more trust in our judgment which allows us to act more rapidly, not second-guess ourselves, and be far more fearless. This trust informs our decision making which creates a far higher likelihood of success. However, if we suffer a setback, the resilience created by our hyper-traits more probably turns the setback into success (or at least a learning experience). Winston Churchill famously observed that "Failure is seldom fatal and success never final—it's courage that counts."

That courage resides in resilience.

---

* The best book on this is *Learned Optimism* by Martin Seligman, Knopf-Doubleday, 2006.

The trust in our own judgment is our gyroscope which keeps us balanced and on a desired route.

Fear Factor

Resilience is more than merely "bouncing back." It's often a matter of bouncing better than ever.

Resilience is apparent in great leaders. Lincoln lost a succession of elections and nominations before becoming the greatest of American presidents. Eisenhower and Allied troops rebounded from a horrible and bloody surprise created by the German offensive known as the Battle of the Bulge. Mohammed Ali returned from brutal losses to Joe Frazier, Ken Norton, and Leon Spinks to reclaim the boxing heavyweight championship.

Steve Jobs returned to Apple after the board ousted him and replaced him with John Sculley to lead the company to its greatest glory ever. Thomas Alva Edison was consistently unable to produce a light bulb—until he did. Actor Reed Birney won the Tony Award for Best Performance by A Featured Actor in A Play for *The Humans* in 2016. In his acceptance speech he said, "The first 35 years in this business were awful!"

If you're not failing, you're just not trying. Failure is a part of growth. But for it to be powerful as a learning experience, we must be resilient. Otherwise, failure seems like a dead end, the final "wall." If we fear failure, then we fear anything that might lead to failure, including risk, tough decisions, confrontation, conflict, experimentation, and innovations. In other words, all of the required characteristics for successful leaders.

We can't enter situations "trying not to lose." We have to face business and life constantly trying to succeed in order to help ourselves and to help others. Since no one is perfect and no one bats one thousand (Babe Ruth led the major leagues in home runs *and* strikeouts, common for power hitters), we need to prepare ourselves to deal with failure positively by rebounding from it consistently.

And that's why we need to establish and sustain resilience.

The Joys and Lessons of Failure

Our mentality has to be that failure is a learning experience. I've pointed out great leaders in business, entrepreneurialism, sports, the military, and politics who have failed only to have reemerged stronger than ever.

Of course, *there are failures who never reemerge.* But my point to you, short of death, is that this is a mental and emotional pivot point, not an external control point.

Serotonin is a compound present in blood platelets which can constrict blood vessels, acting as a stimulator of nerve endings. Serotonin drops after a perceived failure. If you *accept* the fact that you're going to be "down" after a bad experience, then you're more likely to be able to deal with it, having anticipated it. Your funk will be shorter and not as severe.

While we all may prepare ourselves for failure in terms of contingent actions and resilience, we also need to prepare ourselves *for the physiological and emotional aftermaths of failure.*

Having a healthy and well-developed sense of humor helps us to appreciate and learn from failure. If we see ourselves as mere mortals, susceptible to pratfalls and errors, we're able to kid about them when they occur and not regard them as devastating to our self-worth. However, if we tend to be humorless and try to project an image of perfection and unassailable quality, we suffer greatly when that image is dented or even demolished. Think of the meetings where the boss laughed off an error and everyone was relieved, versus those meetings where a boss was furious at everyone present. (Most anger is actually self-anger redirected at others to protect one's psyche.)

If you believe your locus of learning is internal—fixed, in that you have already all the learning you're going to have—failure is very damaging. After all, you can get no better, learn no more. But if you believe your locus of learning is *external*—you can always learn more and grow—then failure is not nearly as threatening (or even not threatening at all). Stanford Psychologist Carol Dweck has done significant research in this area, calling these mindsets which are "fixed" or "malleable."*

Another way to treat failure as a positive is to stop looking for blame and start looking for *cause*. Our fixation on blaming someone (others if we have a borderline personality disorder, or yourself if you're neurotic) distracts us from finding out *why* the failure occurred *so that we can prevent a recurrence in the future.* That kind of positive action encourages our learning from the failure instead of mourning over it or trying to blame it on someone.

We can't control everything. Some issues are out of our control, such as the weather, the tax code, a boss suddenly changing her mind, a subordinate becoming ill, a competitor launching a new technology. It's important to accept the various dynamics of control.

In the lower left quadrant of Figure 5.1 are people who believe there is no control, external or internal. So every day is simply a random walk with no indication of what might happen or why. Obviously, effective leaders never inhabit this quadrant.

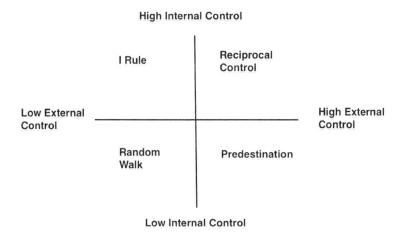

Figure 5.1 *The dynamics of control.*

---

* *Mindset*, Penguin/Random House, 2006.

In the upper left are those who believe that they have total control. This is the motivational speaker shouting at you that you are your own best friend and can control everything in your life. (Never mind that that motivational speakers is often overweight or addicted to tobacco and is talking to you about control.) This is the message in books like *The Secret.*[*]

The leaders in this area are and were people like Napoleon Hill and Bernie Madoff. They thought they were infallible and/or could fool all of the people all of the time. That usually brings either Elba or jail.

In the lower right is a Calvinistic type of predestination, advising us that we have control over *nothing* and that all control is external. These leaders are often seen on the pulpit, immersed in fire and brimstone, telling us that God will take care of everything and we can only pray. Most rational religious people will tell you, however, that God has given us free will, which takes us to the upper right quadrant.

Here we see the reciprocity between external and internal control. We influence the world and it influences us. ("We build our houses and then they build us," observed Churchill, referring to Parliament.) We realize that the weather can affect our plans, but we can choose a rain date or move the event inside. A leader deals with a board that refused to fund an initiative by changing the nature of the alternative.

Finally, failure often calls for us to seek help and not to shoulder the burden ourselves. This is where family, counseling, coaching, and/or colleagues can help tremendously. When we share our angst we also learn more about how to deal with it because trusted others have been down similar roads.

Fear Factor

We never have total control, so fearing its loss is rather pointless.

---

[*] Atria Books, 2006.

Fearless leaders avail themselves of these types of reactions and behaviors in order to turn failure into positive life lessons and even joy, because resilience resides in knowing that you've "come back" time and time again, creating powerful precedents for the future.

Why Worry about What You Can't Control?

The American theologian Rheinhold Niebuhr is credited with writing what's known as The Serenity Prayer:

"God grant me the serenity to accept the things I cannot change, courage to change the things I can, and wisdom to know the difference."

It is commonly used in Alcoholics Anonymous meetings but is not expressly meant for addiction. We seem to be consumed by the need to control in a world, as I've shown, that is one, at best, of reciprocal control. "Acts of God" are written into contracts. "In God We Trust" is on the currency. Congress still begins its sessions with a benediction. "So help me God" ends the vow a witness takes to tell the truth (though there is a progressive move to take God out of there). These are less isolated remnants of past traditions and beliefs than they are pragmatic, contemporary acknowledgments that we are not masters of all we purvey.

One of the positive aspects of an "empty nest" (when your children have left for college or their own jobs, or marriage) is that you simply can't worry like you once did. At one point you stayed awake awaiting their return at night, keeping track of the hour. But once they were away at school, that practice is academic (no pun intended) since you have no idea where they are or until what time, nor could you reasonably expect to find out (without your kids disowning you).

Although it's tough to admit at first, it's a huge relief not to worry about what you can't control.

In leadership, you cannot control (among many other things):

- Competitors' decisions in the marketplace
- Employees' daily, personal actions

- The "grapevine"
- Media reactions to your performance
- Union activities
- Interest rates
- Regulatory rules and changes

I know that you're thinking that you can "influence" these things, but influence isn't control.

I once worked for a company president who insisted on opening all mail himself, despite to whom it was addressed, and passing on a copy to the intended recipient once he cleared it. How obsessive was this? Well, you received copies of Christmas cards! He also went through the trash each evening after employees left the office. This is the obsession and fallacy of control, because people quickly learned how to hide things from him very effectively.

Fear Factor

"Control" is the power to direct the outcome of events and peoples' actions. As they say in Brooklyn, fuggedaboudit!

The key for leaders is not to find new and more convoluted ways to control, but rather to enable new behaviors that allow them not to obsess about control. Here are some suggestions:

- *Focus on outcomes, not tasks:* So long as you achieve the goals you're seeking within legal, ethical, and financial parameters, why not allow yourself some leeway on how to get there? There are always a variety of good avenues to use, each with attendant benefits and risks. It's far easier (and realistic) to manage a team toward a goal using agreed upon metrics for success than it is to try to manage every team member's every task every day.

- *Assume people are healthy and not damaged:* You're hoping that people expect positive and productive behaviors from you, so why not initially expect that from others? Never assume someone is dilatory, or trying to cheat you, or not able to perform *unless you have observed behavior and have environmental evidence to support those beliefs.* When you assume the other person can't or won't perform, you will tend to exert more control whether it's needed or not.

- *Appreciate the difference between skills deficiencies and attitude deficits.* If all indications are that I can do the job but I won't, you're dealing with an attitude problem. You can't "train" me out of an attitude problem. However, if I want to do the job but simply don't know how, you can't "motivate" me to do it without proper skills transfer and tools. Control the proper responses, don't employ improper responses and try harder to control them. (The philosopher Santayana: A fanatic is someone who loses sight of his goals and consequently redoubles his efforts.)

- *Always have a Plan B:* Don't ever launch anything important (personally or professionally) without a fallback plan. I once worked with a business owner who had a key client support person who had client relationships that the owner himself did not have. "What if he leaves?" I asked. "He would never leave," said the owner. He left. Today, that owner has a backup relationship with every key client. *You need to exert control over possibilities that don't yet exist but might.* That's not paranoid. It's called "a contingency."

Stop worrying about what you can't control *and what you shouldn't control.* Mike Tyson pointed out once that every fighter has a plan when he steps into the ring, but it's abandoned once he's hit in the jaw. You're far better off being alert "in the moment" and dealing with what's in front of you. "Loss of control" is critical in a moving vehicle, but even those have automatic pilots and cruise control.

Control your emotions and your responses, and that's a fine condition to be in.

CHAPTER 6

Changing Your Metrics

Our problem is comparing ourselves with the wrong people using the wrong standards. Some batters fear the pitcher so much that they're "out" before they ever take a swing. And some people fear the meeting so much that they lose the sale before they walk in the door.

Never Compare Yourself to Your Cousin

A metric is an indicator of the size and shape of something, and of progress toward a goal. Many management gurus will tell you that if you can't measure something then it's not worth seeking. Metrics can be tricky. Zeno's Paradox observes that if you make progress at the rate of half the distance to your goal every day, you'll never reach your goal.

In most organizations, functions without P&L (profit and loss) responsibility often develop metrics that are, in fact, unmeasurable:

- We'll be more confident we can reach our goals.
- Customers will think more highly of us.
- Our communications will improve.
- The aesthetics of the workplace will be heightened.

And in many cases, the measures are simply deliverables:

- There will be a training program on March 3.
- The meeting will occur as planned each week.
- The report will be delivered on June 1.
- We will address the board with the results at the next meeting.

Personal metrics suffer the same ambiguity and lack of focus:

- I'll be a better partner or spouse.
- I'll be more patient.
- My decisions will involve more people.
- I'll be better presenting at company meetings.

Fear is often present when we use the wrong metrics or no metrics at all. The question to ask is one I learned from Robert Mager, a famed expert in objectives and goal accomplishment. He said, "How would you know it if you tripped over it?" What he meant was simply this: What is the environmental evidence, including observed behavior, that tells me we're making progress toward our goals or have reached them?

Many of our metrics are deceiving, misapplied, and even malicious. Many of you have been in the position of hearing a parent say, "You did well this semester, but your cousin Vinny was making the honor roll at this point." Or, "You played a great game, but cousin Cynthia used to average twice as many goals per game as you do."

So, despite doing well, winning, and even excelling, the metric being applied is that you're not all that good. In other words, you're not winning *enough*.

The converse of this trap is the complacency that accompanies higher position and greater success when we neglect to raise our metrics. ("Raising the bar" is quite popular colloquially, but how do you know it's been raised, and how do you know you're clearing the new height?) We discussed earlier that with each promotion you change your subordinates, colleagues, and superiors. That requires some adjustment to complete those transitions effectively.

Be careful about your avatars—that is, to whom you compare yourself. Frank Sinatra Jr. was a pretty good singer, but not much at all if all you did was compare him to his father and not simply regard his particular body of work. Not every painting has to be by Rembrandt or Velázquez to be brilliant, not every quarterback has to be Tom Brady, not every CEO Jack Welch, not every entrepreneur a budding Steve Jobs.

You shouldn't allow your cousin's performance to be the metric, nor your predecessor, nor your superior, nor anyone else. Too frequently we are comparing ourselves to others in bizarre circumstances, because they operated in a different milieu, had different equipment, or different rules. And when those people are retired and become "legends," it's incredibly difficult to match or exceed their work. *And if they've passed away you can never compare to them at all.*

If you do manage to surpass the old standards, someone will point out that we have better medical care now, or the internet, or faster transportation, or more choices. It doesn't matter, you can't compete against such different circumstances. So your victory still isn't "enough."

Leaders become fearful when they are afraid they cannot match or exceed the metrics expected of them. This, by the way, is why sales people and sales managers consistently "low ball" their forecasts, because they are seeking a lower, easier metric to exceed in order to maximize their bonuses. I recall one of my ace sales people dejected at the end of the year.

"What's wrong?" I asked. "You had a great year and will receive a full bonus?!"

"Right," he said, "but on January 1 I'm a bum again with an even bigger quota to beat."

Never compare yourself to others unless you're actively on a sports field competing in the moment. If you need to catch and pass the person ahead of you, fair enough. But that's not the kind of competition we find in the executive suite.

I ran the sprints in school (it was called "the hundred-yard dash" back then) because it was simple. You crouched in the starting blocks, a gun went off, and you ran like crazy. In ten seconds it was over. You were a winner or not. I simply focused on the tape at the finish line and ran like a wild man, trying to run about ten yards past the tape so that I wouldn't subconsciously let up at the finish.

In track you're taught to *never* look around. You never look over your shoulder or even at the next lane. You focus on the finish line, the ultimate metric, trying to get there first. The great pitcher Dizzy Dean said, "Never look back, someone may be gaining on you."

Create your own measures of progress, speed, and ultimate success. This is not about "one size fits all." And the more they are personalized, the less you'll have to fear.

Excellence Trumps Perfection

You've had successful airline flights, no doubt, or you wouldn't be reading this. But you've never had a perfect one. There have been issues with leaving on time, or the food, or the seat adjustments, or the wait for the lavatory, or a surly flight attendant, or the loss of Wi-Fi.

You've had great meals, but never perfect ones. Something spilled, or the lighting was too bright (or too dim), the server wasn't attentive, the food cooled too quickly, a noisy table of diners was disturbing you. (And you didn't even know what might have been happening in the kitchen before you received your food!)

Perfection is a rare condition. I've always marveled at the subjective scoring in gymnastics and ice dancing, for example, where three judges will give a "ten" score and the Romanian judge will hand out a 7.8. Is it perfect or isn't it?

It's probably not, because nothing is.

Umpires don't always agree with the technological strike zone you can see on television, football referees get pass interference wrong about a quarter of the time, and they've resorted to technology in tennis to determine if a ball is on the line or over it. And the umpire can still overrule that!

But the point is to have a fair game, a great event, a competitive meet. In business, we want a level playing field and an equal starting point. Who finishes first is up to our talents and hard work. But a lot can happen along the way.

If you are expecting perfection in leadership, stop it. We all make mistakes, we all "blow the call" to use a sports term. The issue is, however, are we meeting or surpassing our goals within legal and ethical parameters?

The Patriots won the 2019 Super Bowl by a score of 13–3 over the Rams. Most pundits called it the worst Super Bowl ever, devoid of high scoring and full of errors by both coaches and players. But you don't win for style in football, you win by having more points than the other team at the end of the game. *And the 13–3 score was the Patriots largest margin of victory in any of their six Super Bowl wins!*

Fear Factor

The Olympics may claim that it's not about winning or losing but rather how you play the game, yet they keep a close score of medals won by which countries and play the national anthems only for the gold medal winners. Your investors DO care about success—the "what"—over the "how."

If you seek fearlessness, you have to eschew seeking perfection. The two are anathema to each other.

The effects of chasing perfection are enormously costly. Here are some of the common characteristics:

- Self-editing: We hesitate to say or write something because we feel it can be improved. We waste time in writing without really creating much of an improvement, and we often lose the moment in conversation when the narrative moves on before we've "perfected" our contributions.

- Vacillation: We don't make prompt or crisp decisions. We debate and seek more and more information to the point of paralysis. By the time we are ready the opportunity has passed.
- We abhor risk and overestimate it: Risk is the huge danger to perfection ("The best laid plans oft gang agley...." By Robert Burns), so we try to eliminate risk altogether rather than merely trying to live with it and mitigate its effects. No matter how thorough the fire prevention planning, we still take out insurance and install sprinklers. But perfectionists will keep laboring over more and more far-fetched prevention.
- Consternation over problems and errors: Setbacks are never considered as minor but rather as undermining the perfection that was sought. (Perfectionists have zero resilience, by the way.) Therefore, there is a genuine threat of derailing whenever even a minor glitch appears, let alone a major setback.
- Fear of non-perfectionists: It is difficult to collaborate with or even relate to non-perfectionists because they are so threatening, able to succeed in even high degrees of ambiguity and happily dealing with problems on the fly. A perfectionist will feel either inadequate or highly threatened—or both.

Perfectionism leads to great fear. I've observed consistently that brilliant, fearless leaders have the capacity and willingness to deal with very high degrees of ambiguity, and often thrive in such circumstances. It's like the ability to "free climb" a mountain and not be dependent on ropes and carabiners, or playing an instrument "by ear" rather than through meticulous practice on set pieces.

How do you avoid perfection and become more fearless, freeing yourself of this baggage?

My 80% rule is that when you're 80% ready, MOVE! The final 20% you invest in anything—a book, a speech, a meeting, an evaluation—is pretty much repetitive and overly cautious and non-helpful—*and unappreciated by the audience.* You're better off acting rather than waiting, and adjusting matters while you're on the move. You can see from Figure 6.1

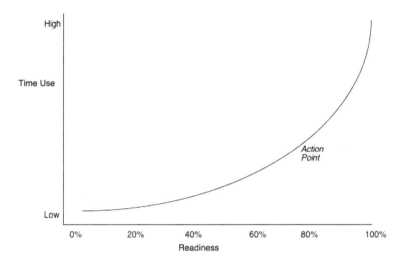

Figure 6.1 *The 80% rule.*

that after 80 percent of readiness, the attempt to reach the final 20 percent is extremely highly labor intensive.

All Things Are Relative, Just Ask the Person behind You

My wife is five feet tall. When she was visiting my office in San Francisco, she asked the three women who worked for me where a mirror might be, since there was none in the rest room. They told her they used the mirror in the stock room next to the door. My wife couldn't find it.

One of them then went back and showed it to her. Since all three women (and I) were 5'9" to 5'11" the mirror was at about five feet, ten inches off the floor. My wife never saw it! (Today, in Global Entry at immigration, the machines don't automatically adjust as they do in other parts of the world, so the photo taken is of my wife's forehead and hair. The immigration guy actually looks at this, shrugs, and lets us through. I am not making this up! Good enough for government work!) Our Bentley has a neck warmer at the top of the seat which merely blows my wife's hair around.

Perspective is everything, especially in fighting fear and being fearless. A pilot is calmer in an emergency because the pilot has control, knows what's happening, and can see the immediate repercussions (feedback) based on corrective measures. The passengers, with no such sense of control, and not even knowing what the pilot is doing, have legitimate and total fear.

Are your hands on the controls gaining immediate feedback about your actions?! Fearlessness requires that you have the proper perspective. If you've ever watched traffic jams start to break up, the cars way up in front are moving (and this occurs even at a red light turning green) but the cars in back are still stopped. If they can't see ahead, the drivers begin to wonder if they'll ever move while the drivers in the front *are moving.*

This means in leadership that you cannot afford to be shielded, or filtered, or buffered by middlemen*, or processes, or protocols. Leaders, to gain the right perspective, must be actively engaged with employees, customers, and other stakeholders.

Fear Factor

The more people with genuine good motives or even malicious motives try to shield you from direct contact with customers and employees, the more your information and perspective will suffer, and the more fearful you should be of inaccurate decisions and reactions.

I was sitting in first class on a Delta flight once and noticed the man across the aisle was receiving far better attention than the rest of us. I asked the flight attendant who he was and, sure enough, he was the CEO of Delta Airlines. "He does this quite often," she said, "to learn firsthand what the experience is like on the airline."

---

* Sorry, but some expressions do not permit gender neutrality. "Middle people" sounds like something from *The Hobbit.*

"Then he ought to be back in coach," I pointed out, "with no one taking care of him, a line for the lavatories, and no meal service." I found out that he was not only well recognized in the system, but also announced his flight schedule! These are empty actions and lead to disastrous conclusions (e.g., the service is excellent and the passengers around me quite happy).

The pivotal point about all things being relative is that leaders *both underestimate and overestimate* the organization's impact and repute. The tendency is to assume customers are happy in the absence of negative feedback, and that absence is caused as much by layers of filters and poor sampling as it is by apathetic customers (the CEO on the Delta flight, for example). But in highly competitive professions and industries, there is also the tendency to believe the competing firms are better and your firm always has to try harder. Some firms have capitalized on this by mocking themselves with their potential customers:

We're number two, so we have to try harder. (Avis Rental Cars)

With a name like Smuckers it has to be good. (JM Smucker Company)

Here are some final points about perspective that can increase the boldness of any leader and dissipate the fear of making bad decisions or taking too long to make them:

- You don't have to be perfect, you only have to be successful.
- People either meet expectations, fail to meet expectations, or exceed expectations. Two of those are good. Don't get caught in dynamics where "you can't win enough" or "we could have done still better."
- Mistakes happen to all of us all the time. Resilience will serve as a course correction.
- If you can make something happen, do it. If you can't, stop worrying about it. Understand the nuances of what you can control, what you can only influence, and what you simply have to accept.

- Use your own metrics to determine your personal and professional progress and success. Don't allow someone else to apply other metrics or, even worse, apply them yourself.
- Put yourself in the other person's shoes and ask yourself what your reaction would be to your service levels, reactions, and performance, both personally and organizationally.*

What's good one time isn't so good another, and what works for someone else may not work for you. Every client is somewhat different, every customer has his or her own needs. Blanket approaches tend to smother flames. Let your light shine.

How to Fearlessly Become Number One

We talked earlier about the "sharp right turn" that helps you create a new market and a higher standing as an industry leader.

Let's talk now about that sharp right turn as an individual leader.†

There is no perfect leadership style. I've never found one. Those who claim they have are usually simply hawking their own approaches and tests and coaching. "Red" or "blue" or "green," High D, Expressive, Inverted, INTJ, hypotenuse—they mean zero, zilch, nada.

The muckraker and author Lincoln Steffens observed, "If we had had good kings we'd all still be monarchists."

There are three keys to leadership which *are* universally applicable and markers of excellence in my experience (in addition to fearlessness, of

---

* I heard somewhere once that the good thing about putting yourself in someone else's shoes before giving them negative feedback is that when they wake up, you'll be miles away and they'll have no shoes.

† There is no political connotation about "right" turn, you can make it "left" turn if you like and, alas, I feel obligated to clarify that in these times.

course), however, and I'm selling you nothing at all in support of them (you've already bought, borrowed, or stolen this book):

1. Consistency: Most if not all of the leadership literature over the past 20 years has preached the power of consistency as a powerful leadership trait. People can work happily for all kinds of (healthy) leadership styles so long as they know what to expect. But if a leader is irritated at a development on one day, and ecstatic about an identical development the next day, people head for the bunkers.

2. Reliability: Outstanding, trusted leaders do what they say they will do. They keep promises. Trust is extraordinarily important in following others, and the only worse thing than no trust from the outset is original trust that's lost. People need to be able to be confident that what they're told is what they'll see.

3. Flexibility: No one style is perfect, but the ability to adapt to different styles is crucial. A leader can't expect employees, peers, customers, superiors, suppliers, and other stakeholders to constantly adjust to his or her demeanor and behaviors. (How can you expect countless others to adjust to you during the day?) Thus, superb leaders understand when to become more or less analytical, more or less deliberate, more or less impatient, and so forth. As Machiavelli observed about leaders long ago, "They suit their conduct to the times."

Ignore the tests and horoscopes, the multiple choice questions, the comparisons such as, "Would you rather be eating rigatoni without silverware or sitting on a cactus?" They're all nonsense.

Instead, consider that it may be the time for you to take that 90-degree turn and adopt a differing set of behaviors. We've said earlier that promotion leads to different relationships with former peers, subordinates, and superiors, requiring a behavior change on your part. But a promotion isn't required to realize that to become a great leader (or a *greater* leader) you sometimes have to change your habits and actions.

You, personally, become a respected and powerful leader when you exhibit these traits and don't bow to popular demand, the easy decision, or delegating what is truly your accountability. Consensus is not equivalent to "quality" and uniformity is a chimera.

There are several ways to demonstrate leadership:

- Reward and punishment. This is the "big stick vs. carrot" approach, which is prehistoric. Big sticks only work as long as they are employed and no one comes along with a still bigger stick. And money provided for unhappy employees merely creates wealthier, unhappy employees.
- Hierarchical power. People obey and follow because they are expected to by dint of your organizationally bestowed power. However, it's easy to subvert such power through procrastination and passive-aggressive behavior, as we've discussed earlier.
- Expertise. People will follow because you're smarter, more experienced, and better-versed than others. But these traits apply to a limited range of content and not for leadership skills, *per se.*
- Referent. This is the charisma factor. I follow you because I'm motivated to do so by your appeal. There is a bearing and demeanor that demands by respect, loyalty, and commitment.

Case Study

The highest percentage of officers killed in the American Civil War was at Brigadier General (one star) rank, because these men mounted a horse and led their brigade of about 2,500 troops against enemy guns, serving as the most vulnerable to enemy fire. People readily followed that kind of courage and example.

Here are the most fearless, personal challenges for a leader who wants to make a mark:

- Fire people who need to be fired because of skill and/or attitude deficits that can't be corrected.
- Never ask anyone to do something you wouldn't or haven't done.
- Share credit for success but take accountability for failure.
- Talk to people directly, not through secretaries or assistants.
- Explain circumstances honestly, especially negative developments, don't use subterfuge.
- Promote, select, and praise strictly on merit.

Fear Factor

Effective leaders receive the benefit of the doubt so that they don't have to continually justify and explain their actions. Such loyalty creates and supports fearless behavior.

Changing your metrics will change your life. Clinging to old metrics will threaten your future.

CHAPTER 7

Organizing Fearlessness

Fear can be an all-embracing life choice, or it can be relegated to its proper, minor role in our lives. Not every mole is melanoma, and losing your car keys doesn't mean you're senile. Fear, like anything that's emotional, can be controlled and sublimated.

Churchill Was Very Accurate but They Still Threw Him Out

I grew weary once of someone claiming she was the "finest dance instructor in the world" when there wasn't a scintilla of evidence to support that claim: She was struggling financially, she had no public brand, professional dancers I knew had never heard of her. She was a legend in her own zip code.

We can't simply prance about proclaiming that we're "fearless leaders." We have to demonstrate that reference and that takes some organizing. No, that's not counterintuitive. We organize ourselves to climb mountains, win at poker, find the right life partner. There are no guarantees, but if you weren't serious about *how* to be a more fearless leader you wouldn't be taking the time to read this book, right?

Winston Churchill served as Conservative Prime Minister from 1940 to 1945—basically the years of the Second World War. He was the brave epitome of the nation during the Blitz, staggering military losses on land, capital ships sunk at sea, and, before Pearl Harbor, near-total isolation after the capitulation of France. With the war won and Franklin Roosevelt dead early in his fourth term as president, Churchill was defeated in the general elections when his party lost. He returned to the post a second time, from 1951 to 1955.

Bravery and courage aren't sufficient for fearless leadership to endure. One must always have the best interests of the public, the employees, and the various other stakeholders in mind. (I've never seen a company with unhappy employees and happy customers, for example.) Being fearless isn't being ruthless, or rash, or headstrong, or aloof.

It's being bold in the interests of others.

Fear Factor

Too many people in leadership are trying too hard not to disappoint or antagonize others, rather than trying to rally them to show them a better future.

As I'm writing this, a GM plant in Lordstown, Ohio, has been "unallocated." That's a snarky attempt to hide a plant closing. It had already cut the second and third shifts over the recent past. Lordstown is a factory town— there is no other work, with the exception of businesses supporting the plant workers, such as restaurants and florists, manicurists and liquor stores.

This plant is highly profitable. But GM's decision is to stop making sedans and focus on even higher profit SUVs and pickup trucks. Thousands of people without much in the way of savings or extended families will lose their jobs. The GM CEO, Mary Barra, was praised by analysts when this decision was made and the stock climbed.

But this was fearful, not fearless leadership. She was fearful, I believe, of not pleasing investors even more than she already was, of the board's governance and focus on results, of the media scrutiny of her.

A more fearless decision would have involved the union at the plant and worked out some way to at least ease the burden on the workers. The "unallocation" was immediate, with the union informed by the personnel director. The move could have been phased over some time period; workers could have been assisted in finding jobs and even relocating; a decent severance could have been provided; the workers could have been asked to be a part of the decision on how to move forward.

That would have been fearless because it would have accommodated *others' legitimate self-interests.* But such concern might have seemed weak to others, questioned by powerful people, criticized by institutional investors. And so a fearful decision was made in which the decision maker and those among the top of the hierarchy were not adversely affected at all. The adverse consequences were rather directed at people who had no say in the matter and who were powerless to combat it.

This might have been an accurate financial decision, but I would still throw her out, *à la* Churchill. It's too easy to make money on the misfortune of others, but it's truly fearless when you refuse to do that and find another way, even if it means criticism of one's actions.

Don't forget, during his long, successful tenure at GE, Jack Welch went from "Neutron Jack" (only the buildings were left standing) to an executive who was considered highly responsive to people and open to critique. *That* was his fearless leadership transition.

Steve Jobs founded Apple, was booted out as CEO, and then triumphantly returned. Bill Belichick failed as head coach of the Cleveland Browns but became what may be the best football coach in history with the New England Patriots. Eisenhower was a questionable senior general with relatively little combat experience when he was placed in charge of the European Theater of Operations to lead the invasion of Normandy. Louis Gerstner Jr. was an unprecedented "outsider" brought into a careening IBM who righted the ship, moved toward consulting revenues, and brought prestige back to the company. Eddie Lampert, the former CEO of a declining Sears, returned to buy it and is reducing it into a shadow of itself, still not immune from bankruptcy.

Fearless leadership isn't about betting the family farm, or being "tough," or making headlines. I don't consider Elon Musk to be a fearless leader so much as a conman, using other people's money and government subsidies to try to keep Tesla afloat amidst bad decisions and quality problems. Fearless leadership is the ability to *help others to thrive, thereby thriving yourself.*

It's not about selfishness but, perhaps counterintuitively, about generosity and synergy.

When to Hold, When to Fold, When It's Gold

When does fearlessness become wild-eyed gambling or intransigent stubbornness? And when is "fearlessness" engaged only with issues such as where to place the vending machines in the cafeteria but not about new product development or anything substantive?

"Fearless" means "lacking fear." As I've explainer earlier, it doesn't mean being blind to issues that might cause one to fight, to have fright, or to engage in flight. Nor does it mean to fool yourself into thinking that fearlessness is sufficient to defeat any rival, to overcome any challenge, to stand fast and think the approaching tornado will spare you.

Some people believe they will occasionally pull the right card for the "inside straight" and some others think it will happen rarely, while others still think it will never happen. What determines which person is wiser or more fearless? *It depends upon the wager, the probabilities, and what you're prepared to lose.*

I enjoy gambling within my budget. If I win, it's gravy, and I know I've won because at a certain point in the winning I stop. If I lose, again within my budget, it's been entertainment, nothing different from allocating money to see a play or go skiing.

But I never gamble at a casino with the intent of winning over the long haul. That's because the odds are indisputably and immutably against me, and I know that. Expecting to make a living by beating a casino is an exercise in denying reality.

I have taken risks with new product offerings, knowing that in the worst case, if I have to withdraw or cancel the offer because of poor receptivity, I can tolerate that financially. I've taken risks with weather, knowing that my "Plan B" can be to move an event indoors or postpone it without great inconvenience or loss. However, if the weather forecast is for thunderstorms, I know in advance to cancel. And if the forecast is for bright sun, I also know that weather forecasts can be wrong.

Hence, the dictum: Hope for the best, prepare for the worst.

Another adage is not to "throw good money after bad." We see this done with people (in the casinos or in business) who irrationally feel their luck is about to change if they simply keep betting on their favorite number or pet project. "In for a dime, in for a dollar" is a clever phrase but a potentially disastrous leadership philosophy.

Fear Factor

Fearless leaders know when to cut their losses.

You have to know when to "fold your hand," and when fearlessness is displayed in a bold *acceptance* of defeat or setback, and further acceptance of the responsibility, as opposed to a belligerent and intractable insistence that things will get better if we just "stay the course."

Believe me, they won't, and the course will deteriorate. Brute force, physically, emotionally, or psychologically, isn't sufficient in most cases in management. *If that were untrue, Sisyphus would be on top of the hill and Picket's Charge would have won the Civil War at Gettysburg.*

Here are fearless criteria to consider when you're evaluating risk, willing to "take a chance," and deciding where the line is between brave and batty:

- Can people be irreparably hurt? You can change the setting on a machine, readjust a thermostat, or press a different button, but you can't take back or erase damage to people any more than you can un-ring a bell. Lower your risk-taking if people's reputations, income, future prospects, or self-worth will be threatened. It's fine to make people uncomfortable, of course, and to shake them up, but not to do harm that could have been foreseen and avoided.

- Is there a viable Plan B or even Plan C that can be ready? Are you engaged in "all or nothing" risks, or can you ameliorate the downside? Can you withdraw an offer or a product quickly, or provide an alternative to an unhappy client? Can you replace people who depart quickly and cost-effectively? In other words, can you move the picnic inside, or are you in a field in the middle of Kansas without any cover for 20 miles?

- What is the reputation factor? The standard question is, "How would you feel about this being reported in the *Wall Street Journal* tomorrow? The people engaged in the college admissions scandals in 2019 certainly didn't consider this issue as they were dropped from their positions, deals were terminated, and the public was disgusted with their fraudulent activity. Will you lose trust and standing that will be impossible to reclaim short term (or even longer term)?

- What are the total financial implications? Is the investment coming from monies not required for other needs? Are the projections reliable and vetted, and has due diligence been performed? Will credit ratings and banking relationships be affected? What will be the impact on investors, present and future? Are regulatory statutes being observed?

These considerations, especially in discussion with trusted others, will help you define the true risk/reward ratio. (See Chapter 3 for the risk/reward assessment diagram.) They are intended to insert rationality and logic into decisions which are too often purely emotional. I've seen companies make acquisitions based purely on some burning ego need to do so, rather than any intelligent business reason.

Finally, when are you "golden," in that your fearlessness is not only appropriate but can exploit an increasingly positive development or circumstances? Any time you see high growth, don't just pat yourself on the back, exploit it. High growth in personal computers and then smart phones prompted accessories, from cases to applications. High growth in personal riding services (Lyft, Uber, et. al.) created frequent rider points, rating systems, tipping options, and so forth.

"Exploit" is not a dirty word, it means "to make full use of something." Make full use of your best results from fearless leadership. Just make sure you can accurately differentiate them from average or even losing hands. Make bold bets only when you know you have a strong hand. Bluffing is not fearless, it's mindless.

The Fearless Posture

When I watch people who have had professional dance training walk across a room in street clothes, they invariably have a certain carriage in their walk. Their posture is erect, their movements graceful and intentional. Their learning and practice of movement are not confined to the dance floor or ballet.

They are part of their being.

Fearless leadership has a "posture," a carriage that is not donned solely during working hours but is a part of one's being. We talked earlier about charisma and referent leadership. "I'll know it when I see it" is a phrase often employed to explain that certain traits hard to conceptually describe are nonetheless obvious when experienced.

These are the hallmarks of fearless leaders as they are observed and interact with others. They aren't temporary, they are permanent.

1. Composure and calmness under pressure

    Counterintuitively, fearlessness is not about the tendency to immediately react. When people "knee-jerk" and feel so panicked that they seize on the first possible action, that is actually a sign of the fear of inaction. Yet airline pilots faced with threats at 36,000 feet calmly go through checklists and manuals before deciding on corrective action. Air Force pilots and astronauts have been lauded for having "the right stuff," popularized in the book of that name by Tom Wolfe, and meaning that they never panic, but always are calm in the face of threatening calamity. It's hard to "shake" or threaten a fearless leader into rash actions.

2. Belief in finding cause and not blame

Fearless leaders waste no time trying to find scapegoats. They immediately seek to find the cause of problems and resolve them, making sure the customers or clients are treated well in the process. If someone must be retrained, admonished, or terminated, that will come in due course. But the first priority is to solve the problem and safeguard the business relationships.

This includes transparency and candor, especially with the media. Neither Volkswagen nor Wells Fargo exhibited such honesty in their infamous problems (fuel emission falsification for the former, and phony client accounts with the latter). Initial leadership decisions were to try to extend the coverup, to deny there was a systematic deception. The result was even more disastrous than the original misdeeds.

Fearless leaders admit to failures and errors and correct them, publicly.

3. Commitment and non-equivocation

There's a bet on the craps tables called "crap check" and it's usually used by the shooter to protect the bet. That is, shoot a craps (2, 3, 12) and the $25 bet is lost, but the craps check costs $5 and approximately repays the lost money. Of course, if you don't shoot a craps then you're out the $5.

Fearless leaders don't engage in "craps checks." They don't try to cover themselves. A "Plan B" is fine in terms of a backup, as is resilience in recovery. But fearlessness is not about protecting yourself as the priority. William Penn observed once, "No pain, no palm; no thorns, no throne; no gall, no glory; no cross, no crown."

You commit to a course of action and don't keep "testing the wind," or bending to public tastes, or investor sensitivity. You do what you believe is right and you accept the fact that some others won't.

4. Listening to the right sources

I cited earlier, "Who are you going to believe, me or your lying eyes?!" Fearless leaders don't heed the grapevine, schoolyard gossip, fake news, or rumor. They consult with experts inside and outside the organization to obtain reliable feedback and ideas, and then make independent decisions. Fearless leaders see coaches as signs of strength, demonstrating the confidence to seek continued growth and improvement. Weak leaders eschew coaching because they believe it shows they are flawed.

Fearless leaders do not heed human resources in their organizations in terms of big picture thinking and strategy, but use it (if at all) for ground-level implementation. Human resources usually touts meaningless training programs and "feel good" initiatives that have zero impact on the nature and direction of the enterprise. HR should handle transactions (relocation, compensation) when not more effectively outsourced altogether, but never transformations, for which they have neither the skills nor the stomach.

5. Making tough calls

Finally, fearlessness is about the backbone, *the posture*, to make the tough and unpopular decisions. That might mean terminating a popular employee who's not performing, changing a policy that costs the company too much money to support, bringing in "outsiders" because their talent is needed, and holding subordinates' feet to the fire for their accountabilities.

Fear Factor

No one in organizations believes what they read or what they hear from senior management. They only believe what they see.

Fearless leaders don't seek to win popularity contests or have the highest survey scores on some HR survey *du jour*. They understand their role is to walk their talk and talk their walk; to be an exemplar and avatar; and to make it clear that the right thing trumps the popular thing wherever the two are in conflict.

The "posture" or carriage of a fearless leader is one of alertness, confidence, and trust in his or her own judgment. It's about self-mastery and not reliant on others' feedback, no matter how well-intentioned.

Fearless leaders walk with the grace of trust in their judgment and belief in their own talent.

Home Is Different from Work, or It Had Better Be

A part of organizing fearlessness is to understand the differing environments and aspects of your life. We don't really have a business life and a personal life, of course, we simply have *a life*. However, there's a non-porous/porous aspect to it, where some things cross the line and others don't (or at least shouldn't).

The latter is often called "compartmentalization," and it's useful for trauma, failure, isolated incidents, and other non-recurring events and situations. Many of us have lost pets, expectedly and unexpectedly. All of us who own dogs, for example, know their life expectancies are far too short, one of God's few errors.

Some people who lose their pet become totally traumatized. I knew a successful business owner who was seriously telling friends that her dog's death was prompting her to just sit by the ocean all day, close her business entirely, and think about her sadness. Having suffered these losses myself, I advise people to immediately get another dog, through which your prior dog's spirit will live on. (I have a weekly comic strip about two of my past dogs called "The Adventures of Koufax and Buddy Beagle," now at over 500 strips. You can find it on my blog at alanweiss.com.)

Anything in life that causes such trauma should be compartmentalized. When my father passed away at 99 years and 11 months, I told my sister

I couldn't immediately return home for the funeral because I was starting a program with a dozen people from all over the world who had paid $15,000 each. I could neither simply send them home (even if I refunded the money) nor could I allow my father's death to impede my helping them. There was nothing I could do, after all, for my father at that point, and the grieving could wait until later.

Thus, my "one life" maxim has some exceptions, such as compartmentalizing trauma in your personal life *and trauma at work.* Losing a key business contract shouldn't cause you to beat your kids (or the dog). Having an argument at work shouldn't monopolize the rest of the week with your family.

And fearlessness means being sensitive to your surroundings and relationships. Most of us have heard on more than one occasion from a spouse or partner, "You know, you're not at work right now"!

There are other environments to consider, as well: clubs, social gatherings, civic meetings, holidays, vacations, volunteer work, philanthropy, and so on. We need to adjust our behavior so that "fearlessness" includes changing the emotional rheostat at given times and under certain conditions.

Being fearless is not being ruthless, or uncaring, or intransigent. It's about not being afraid to appropriately change your behavior based on varied situations and conditions.

For example, in Latin America it's quite common for meetings to begin an hour late, and if you're invited to someone's home for dinner, never to show up on time, because your host will be in the shower. It's also rare to hear a blatant "no," but rather a soft "yes" that really doesn't mean anything. It's just a polite way of not saying "no."

Case Study

A former marine captain was a top administrator at our kids' private school. He believed, apparently, that he was still in the military and still giving orders to parents, staff, and students.

We were volunteers, about a dozen of us, serving food at a fund raiser, when he marched over and said, "You need to work faster, this line isn't moving out here! These people need food!"

I said to him that he could either start serving food himself or shut up, we weren't his troops. He visibly shook for a moment, but realized he really had no authority, no bars on his shoulders.

Years later, when he passed away, I had no interest in attending the brief service they held at school. He was a leader who wanted to be feared, and I found that reprehensible.

Thus, you adapt to the culture you find yourself in, whether geographically or locally, whether business or home. You may make tough decisions all day long with great effectiveness at work, but that doesn't mean you have to choose the restaurant, the table, and the wine if you're out with friends that evening.

At least, not if you want to keep the friends.

Fear Factor

Truly confident people can change behaviors and allow for vulnerability or uncertainty at appropriate times. You may be certain about expanding into Europe at work, but that doesn't mean you must insist on your vacation spot when discussing it at home.

No one wants to see an airline pilot who notices a warning light on the console to go running down the aisle shouting, "We're doomed!" But we don't mind the airline pilot who says to friends, "You choose the movie, I'm happy to see any of the recommendations." You don't always have to be in charge, you don't always have to consult an instruction manual.

Fearless leaders know when to adjust their behaviors. They don't have to be the center of attention all the time, don't have to have their egos massaged continually.

They're bold when they need to be, and are fearless about that. But they also adapt to the circumstances. The famous video of Steve Balmer, then CEO of Microsoft, screaming like a madman at a company conference, was frightening because he was acting in front of his employees as if in the midst of some cataclysmic fit, yelling and gesticulating as if possessed. This was one of the most aberrant departures from proper executive demeanor I've ever seen. (You can watch it on YouTube here: https://www.youtube.com/watch?v=I14b-C67EXY). This was some attempt to prove himself "hip" or to cater to the crowd that went wildly awry because he was attempting to be someone he is not.

Fearlessness mean unflappability, a phlegmatic attitude that maintains an even keel. Ask yourself how well you handle:

- Unexpected events: Are you panicked or do you calmly study what's occurred?
- Employee uproar: Do you stubbornly back a contentious policy or offer to discuss it with those most affected?
- Customer alienation: Do you desperately slash prices or determine whether the departing customers may not actually be worth trying to lure back?
- Financial reversals or goals not met: Do you radically seek to reduce expenses or find alternative ways to raise revenues?
- Stubborn problems: Do you find someone to blame or gather together objective problem solvers?

I could go on, but you get the picture. Employees want to follow leaders who never panic and who place all developments, no matter how abrupt, into perspective. Customers want to buy from companies whose leadership is reliable and can navigate through any storms. And investors look for leadership which can create new approaches when old ones fail, and not panic.

Finally, the media prefers stories about colossal failures and loss of trust, and you want to stay out of that particular spotlight!

CHAPTER 8

Your Fearless Future

Why is it that when you finally get on the roller coaster, it's seldom your final trip? The "high" of overcoming fear and the confidence will ensue in all aspects of your life. Converting the guy on your shoulder to your personal weapon against fear is vital.

Maintaining a Fearless Demeanor

Leaders serve as avatars. If you want to change the "culture" in an organization, simply change the behaviors of the people to whom others look as exemplars—both formally (hierarchically) and informally (performance).

Fear Factor

"Culture" is that set of beliefs which governs behavior. Change the beliefs and you'll change the behavior.

When people see those in responsible positions cheat or lie or avoid accountability, they feel that such traits and behaviors are the best ways in which to succeed. When they see honesty, and acceptance of accountability, and fearlessness, then they believe that's the way to behave. If you're thinking that this is very simple, you're right. Consulting and coaching are based on common sense, not intricate models and exasperating meetings.

We think of "walking the talk" as behaving in a way that is consistent with what we claim as our values (respecting the customer, collaboration, accepting responsibility, and so forth). However, the converse is also important—"talking the walk." That means that we should be communicating with others *so that they are aware that we are behaving in ways consistent with our values.* This may be publicizing community support and involvement, recognizing high performers, acknowledging mistakes and corrective actions taken, and citing contributions

Case Study

I was visiting our veterinarian with our dogs and waiting for my bill. I was glancing through the Merck Manual about pet health and pharmaceuticals when the vet noticed me. I said, "Merck is a major client of mine, and I've worked with their animal health division."

He said, with moist eyes, "Do you know that Merck has done more for animal health than any other company in history worldwide?" I didn't know that.

The next time I addressed the animal health division personnel I mentioned this encounter. The room was totally silent, and I thought I had made a mistake in recounting it. But later a vice president told me, "These people only hear about delayed shipments, or adverse side effects, or the need for different dosages. They never hear anything like you told them, and they were stunned."

The company needed to "talk its walk" much more, and we arranged for people from the division to meet with veterinarians and to invite those doctors in to future meetings, as well.

When you communicate you provide two simultaneous messages: One is the content of your message, and the other is the process with which it's given. You may think of it as "steak" and "sizzle," the way that many professional speakers do.

Your demeanor—your behavior which is informed by your beliefs and attitudes and is their manifestation—should be positive and admirable. You should display humor when it's appropriate, enthusiasm when required, and somberness when called for. You don't tell a joke about a death, but you also shouldn't give a eulogy in trying to convey a success.

I watched a vice president of a client company on a stage addressing several hundred employees. Visualize the following, *with a monotone, soft, uninflected delivery:*

"I, ah, want to inform you—to tell you—that the, ah, result of the year were somewhat beyond our, er, expectations and plans. Therefore, I'm, ah, here today to tell you that the so-called 'bonus pot,' more properly known as the, ah, employee financial incentive sharing plan, is full, so the, er, bonuses will be fully forthcoming, but not maybe for another week or so."

An employee standing nearby asked me, "Are we being fired?"

Demeanor is both consistent and situational. That is, fearless leaders are assertive and clearly "in charge," but they readily make adjustments for the situation. Sometimes a subordinate has to have the limelight. Sometimes someone could be a bit crisper but is good enough for the circumstances.

I was coaching a CEO in the pharma industry whose habit was to cut off his subordinates in team meetings. I recorded this and played it back for him.

"Oh, right!" he said proudly, I'm showing them that I know the answer and that they're on the right track, or that they're heading in the wrong direction and need reorientation."

"Why don't you allow them to determine that once they're done and dialogue begins?" I asked. He wasn't domineering, he was a fine leader, but he was emphasizing speed over development. I had to explain that just because he could do something better and faster doesn't mean that he should. In an emergency, perhaps, but not in daily interactions.

A prophet is not without honor except in his native place and among his own kin and in his own house. —The Gospel of Mark 6:4

Thus, "demeanor" is situationally dependent. Fearless leaders don't metamorphize into supplicants, but they are flexible enough to become listeners. They don't have to sit at the head of every table.

Dealing with Volatility and Disruption

One of the first insights for fearless leadership is that volatility and disruption are not all that volatile and disruptive. They are the new normal.

Once upon a time, a 50-point move in the Dow Jones Industrial Average would have stopped the presses. Today, a 500-point move doesn't even stop someone's reading. As speed increases and technology becomes more sophisticated, we find ourselves embroiled in greater speed, instantaneous communication, records being broken, tolerances being smaller, and shock being far lower.

Scientists discover distant planets that might support life or begin to understand the workings of a black hole millions of lightyears away, and it's on page 12 of the daily paper. Tom Brady is a six-time Super Bowl winner at age 42. Ho hum. We can be diagnosed through tele-health and our smart phones. Okay. Autonomous cars? Why not?

If we sit in a small boat in the water, we'll be rocked by the wake of every boat passing by, even sailboats. If we are propelled through the water, we can compensate for others' waves and create some of our own. And if we are in a large boat with an intelligent course and able to navigate and make adjustments, we cause others to compensate for us.

"If one does not know to which port one is sailing, no wind is a good wind," observed Seneca.

Fearless leaders don't react to volatility and disruption, they create it. I don't mean that in any kind of malicious sense. I mean that they create new directions and often radical change. (See the sharp right turn we discussed earlier.) IBM makes most of its money today from consulting, not hardware or software. Cars today are driven not so much by engineering as by software—and when they're serviced, the first thing the "mechanic" does is plug in a laptop under the dashboard to obtain a diagnostic report. Every month I receive on my computer a report on every aspect of my Corvette's performance and status, right down to the percentage of time before the oil should be changed based on my driving experience.

Thus, creating change (volatility) and radical new initiatives (disruption) are not malicious moves but rather fearless ones. One of the reasons that architects in the United States have had far lower increases in compensation than all other professional groups is that they have remained in the rut of charging hourly rates to provide blueprints and plans while general contractors and engineers have moved into their space providing more varied services. Higher education and specialty does not necessarily produce boldness, and often results in the opposite—arch conservatism.

In considering your company and your life, how often and to what extent are you considering change rather than merely fixing problems? How often do you willingly take risk rather than protect the status quo? You don't need a hundred people in some "skunk works" to create fresh ideas and new initiatives. You need an environment where there is freedom to fail and the philosophy of making those waves instead of merely dipping your toes into the water.

What areas, strategically and/or operationally, are most likely to provide you with the potential for powerful, profitable disruption? Here are my nominations:

- The global village. There are six billion or so people in the world and they are all potential consumers, especially when they can purchase remotely on credit. Right now, in some remote Indian villages without all of the requisite civic advantages or even normal municipal service of larger towns, local people order everything from shoes to toothpaste using the internet, and products are delivered promptly by capitalistic entrepreneurial firms, faster than the government could ever provide anything.

- The rising middle class. America's poor are wealthier than any other such cohort in the world. Middle classes are rising dramatically in China, where the government is in a frenzy to please such people because they constitute the only solid tax revenues for a country still oriented toward central state welfare. In 2018, all eight major world economies were in some phase of growth, which is quite rare, and while it may not last, is nonetheless symptomatic of synergistic economic growth.

- The emergence of Africa. As the old dictators are replaced or die off, most of Africa will represent a great potential for investment in infrastructure as well as consumer goods. The Chinese have attempted this, but have too often run out of funds leaving local governments with excessive debt. Mutually beneficial private sector partnerships surely seem a logical endeavor here.

- Personal technology. The relationship between ease of purchasing and making a purchase is very strong. Instead of having a card swiped, we could insert it with a chip, and now just breeze it by in the wind. We no longer need to sign the charge. Amazon and Staples, to name just two monster retailers, usually deliver whatever you order online within 48 hours or sooner, and Amazon is focusing as I write this on rapid meal deliveries residentially. How easy can you make it for people to quickly buy and have something delivered? And if you think that's limited to small purchases, there are huge car "vending machines" extant, where you use a credit card to buy the car that then is immediately delivered by ramp or elevator.

- Automated health. Just as your car's (or phone's) navigation system and apps tell you where to turn, when to avoid traffic via detour, and find restaurants or gas stations, a personal navigator (already beginning on some watches) will keep you on your diet, remind you when to eat, calculate calories, suggest when and how to exercise, and alert you when to contact a physician for anomalies (your heart beat is erratic, or that mole is questionable). We think today that walk-in, store-front clinics are breakthrough, but they will disappear just as the physician's house call is seen as a stegosaurus.

You should be facilitating meetings among your team about proactive, conscious, market-domineering disruption and volatility. This should be a regular pursuit no less than financial management or customer contact. You may think that doing so makes these issues "normal" and "routine."

Well, that's because they already are.

Taking the Blow

"You win some, you lose some, and some get rained out, but you have to suit up for them all," observed baseball pitching legend Satchel Paige, who played in his final major league game at age 59.

Fearless leadership implies not being afraid of failure, setback, criticism, or even catastrophe. We've spoken about the need for resilience and that if we're not failing we're not trying. However, we need to look beyond the clichés and motivational slogans on the wall and understand that there is another element here that we need to accept.

Loneliness.

It's one thing to be on a losing team where everyone rallies and says, "We'll get them next time," or "We're all in this together." Yet despite the talk of a "top management team" and sharing credit, it's lonely at the top *and it should be*. Great leaders do not make decisions by committee and don't foist the blame for defeats on others (although they readily share the credit for victories).

Great and fearless leaders have to take the blow.

We often do hear about "taking one for the team," which represents someone making a personal sacrifice for the good of all others. That's not what I'm referring to here. I'm talking about preparing for and accepting the fact that leaders will sometimes be excoriated by the press, blamed by employees, vilified by shareholders, and even rejected by family members. That may be a bit bleak, but there is a piranha-like feeding frenzy when something goes wrong *and everyone seeks blame instead of cause.* The blame always starts at the top, and when it is denied at the top—as we've seen by Volkswagen, Tesla, and Wells Fargo CEOs to name just a few—the blame merely intensifies and the disavowals are looked upon as representing poor character and suspicious motives (which is an accurate reaction).

Case Study

I recently had a set of poor experiences at a major hotel in Washington, DC, where I'd conducted programs in the past. I wrote a note to the general manager and told him I thought he'd want to know.

He wrote back the next day and told me what actions he was taking, apologized, told me he'd like to personally handle my next visit, and then said, *I take full responsibility for what occurred and I will personally ensure it doesn't happen again.*

He took the blow.

Here are the realities:

1. Fearless leadership involves prudent risk taking.
2. We share credit but accept blame ourselves, personally.
3. We will not always be accurate or correct or successful.
4. We will, therefore, receive both appropriate and inappropriate criticism.

5. Resilience is a key recovery mechanism.
6. Nevertheless, we must accept public and private negative reactions.

Fear Factor

If we're always right and never fail, then we're not fearless, we're fearful (because we've been very conservative). Therefore, be prepared to fail and accept the consequence yourself.

"The buck stops here" was the aphorism made famous by President Harry Truman. I've found it to be somewhat disingenuous, in that the ultimate decision and courage has to be shown much farther down the line. Non-commissioned officers commanding troops on the front lines of battle win the wars, not officers and civilians sitting in Washington.

Fearless leadership has to encourage people at all levels to "take the blow." What does that mean? It means a front desk clerk says she's sorry to a customer who points out that her reservation was mishandled. The clerk doesn't call for a manager and doesn't say, "That's a different department." She admits it was her organization's fault and moves immediately to correct it.

The FedEx delivery person giving you a banged-up package apologizes for it and doesn't blame some other driver, or the sorting people in Memphis, or someone in the back office. He points out the damage, apologizes, and asks the customer if he'd like to fill out a damage claim form on the spot.

Every time an unhappy customer tells a front-line company representative that he or she wants to talk to a supervisor or manager, several things are guaranteed to occur:

- The person will talk to someone else.
- Time to resolve the problem increases.

- Cost to resolve the problem increases.
- The customer will get some concession, ranging from a slight discount to waiving of all charges.

So, why not give lower-level people the empowerment to "take the blow"?

Case Study

Years ago, Ritz-Carlton Hotels granted every employee the right to spend up to $2,500 to resolve a customer's complaint of unhappiness. ("Backstage" the hotels had signs in employee areas: "We are ladies and gentlemen serving ladies and gentlemen.") The money might be applied to a free drink or even a room night.

When Marriott took over Ritz-Carlton, one could see an instant decline, from the less expensive amenities in the bathroom to a lack of personally escorting guests who needed directions. And they did away with the $2,500 because of the fear that employees would spend $1,000 to please a guest when $25 would have been sufficient. Marriott successfully brought Ritz-Carlton down to its brand level, instead of maintaining a leading edge, top-end brand.

You've no doubt realized that "taking the blow" means accepting accountability and, for the fearless leader, empowering others to accept that accountability and "take the blow" when necessary.

There are few traits as powerful as that which enables someone to say, "This is our fault and I will rectify it. What will make you happy?"*

---

* A fascinating aspect of customer psychology is that when you ask someone to tell you what will make things better they almost invariably choose something less than you would have offered without their input. That may have been Marriott's legitimate worry, but that didn't justify ending the empowerment entirely.

Constant Recovery and Success

The more you've been successful the more successful you'll be. Similar to motor skills (you never "forget" how to ride a bike), mental skills can become ingrained. When we're accustomed to success we realize that we're likely to be successful again, not without interruption, most of the time.

However, to move this from "unconscious competency" to "conscious competency" we have to remind ourselves about *why* we've been successful. We have to be able to replicate the *causes* of our success. No one who's successful in business, entertainment, sports, politics or any other pursuit begins with a simplistic notion of simply "winning." They have a "game plan" or a set of activities they know will support their winning in most situations.

A bull market is not defined by ever-increasing highs. It's defined, rather, by increasing highs accompanied by lows *which themselves are constantly higher.* In other words, there are losses, but not as severe as in the past. Even the lows are higher, if that makes sense.

Fearless leaders have setbacks, reversals, and failures. We've discussed the need for resilience at length earlier. But the key element here is that the failures are not catastrophic, not as bad as past setbacks, and thus the leadership is like a bull market in that, while it varies and has highs and lows, overall it's constantly surging ahead. Warren Buffet, Steve Jobs, Bill Gates, Jack Welch, Bill Belichick, Winston Churchill, Oprah Winfrey—all of them made mistakes as they continued to drive their enterprises upward and onward.

These recoveries and successes are closely linked to your self-esteem and its constancy. You should never allow yourself to be as high as your last success or as low as your last setback. That kind of huge swing turns you into a pendulum. You should have a constant self-esteem that enjoys victories and weathers defeats, as you can see in Figure 8.1.

If you watch the truly great athletic teams (or even individual performances), you find that they sometimes have to engage in startling "comebacks" when they're behind. I saw the Boston Celtics win a game once when

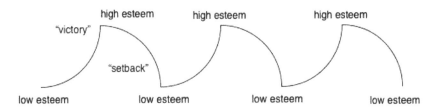

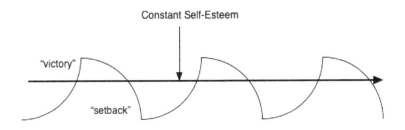

Figure 8.1   *The constancy of healthy self-esteem.*

behind and only a tenth of a second remaining in the contest. The New England Patriots beat the Atlanta Falcons in the Super Bowl after being down by 25 points late in the third quarter. The Boston Red Sox won the World Series after trailing the Yankees three games to zero in the best-of-seven event.

Fear Factor

Fearless leadership is at its best and is most felt when times are tough and things are rough.

When you talk to the players on these victorious teams after their comeback, they all say approximately the same thing: "We never doubted we would win." These are people who are confident in themselves but also highly confident in their leadership, whether the quarterback, the coach, the manager, or informal team leaders.

We see the same phenomenon among sales teams behind in their quotas, construction crews behind in their operations, students who do poorly in some exams. If you've bounced back before, you can bounce back again. Not everyone leads "wire to wire."

Fearless leaders recognize that being at less than optimal performance is merely another situation to be confronted and improved, not a staggering blow. Hence, constant recovery is about these elements:

- Never being surprised by being behind
- Exuding the confidence that you can surmount the setback
- Staying calm and never panicking
- Living and exemplifying a resilient existence

Case Study

Mercedes-Benz of North America asked me to find out what their competitors were doing because they were constantly receiving higher service scores on independent surveys than was Mercedes. I suggested that we start "at home" and asked if there were Mercedes stores (that's what they called the dealerships) that were better on service than others.

There certainly were, so I started with them because I figured we could certainly raise standards *within* the company to what was the current best. And at the first and highest rated dealer I visited, Viti Mercedes in Tiverton, Rhode Island, I quickly found my answers.

The owner at that time, Nick Viti, told me that problems were the key to his success. When a customer complained, Viti Mercedes did everything possible to delight that customer. For example, if the new buyer of an $80,000 car came back the next day and pointed out a scratch on the fender, the Viti people apologized, provided a Mercedes loaner, and fixed the scratch for free, no questions asked.

At other dealers I was to visit, they asked that same customer how the customer managed to scratch the car so quickly after purchase, and cited $800 to refinish and repaint the damage.

The total actual labor and materials came to about $200 at the time.

And remember this: Referral business and repeat business are the heart and soul of the automotive business, and perhaps, yours.

I've always told people I coach that a question or complaint *is a sign of interest*. What we don't want is apathy, with customers or audiences simply disappearing. We want critique and argument and complaint so that we can engage and develop trusting relationships.

No one I've ever known comes home from a trip and raves that the hotel room service was delivered on time, or the ballpark sold beer and hot dogs. People DO remark when something goes wrong and isn't expected, and then is made better with a free dinner or a free beer or even a sincere apology.

Fearless leaders are proficient in good times and bad, with successes and problems, because their ego and esteem are constant. They don't get carried away by victory and aren't knocked cold when they have to take a blow.

They soldier on.

The Guy on Your Shoulder Redux

I had suggested way back in Chapter 1 that you flick the superego, anthropomorphic little guy off your shoulder and crush him. You need to eliminate the little voice that constantly casts doubt, represents some impossible, idealized future, and spends the day trying to ensure that you know you're not good enough no matter what you achieve.

I wanted to end this book by revisiting the concept in a counterintuitive fashion. That is, I want you to create your own little guy who makes his living by consistently reminding you about how good you are. The intent here is to be consciously competent of your strengths and assiduously pursue their application.

You need a fearless coach on your shoulder.

This is not about an acid trip or carrying around a munchkin from *The Wizard of Oz*. I don't expect you'll talk to the guy, at least in public. But I do expect that, if you create him correctly, he'll talk to you at all the most important junctures of your life and career. He's there to remind you that you've conquered challenges before, bounced back from defeats, turned setbacks into victories, and allowed unjust criticism to wash down the drain.

We're all very unconsciously competent at slogging through our defeats and dissecting them until we're pretty much depressed. That's why we need conscious competency to remind us of our assets and power. Of course, you may choose to make notes or talk to yourself in the mirror or make periodic affirmations.

But I favor the little guy perched up there with a panoramic view and great perspective whispering about our strengths.

Here's how you create this guy, this ongoing reminder of fearlessness, trust in your judgment, and admirable behavior:

- Remind yourself daily of things you've accomplished that you're quite proud of. Use several so it's clear that there is no "luck," no "fluke" involved in your successes.
- Remind yourself daily of the traits that have accounted for your success and which are as strong as, or stronger than, they ever were. These might be your use of language, critical thinking skills, resilience, risk assessment, and so on.
- Use an "upside/downside" (reward/risk) ratio to ensure that your risk taking is prudent and not a gamble and is aligned with probable, pragmatic, positive outcomes.
- Be careful about receiving advice. Don't consider unsolicited feedback (which I've noted is always for the sender) but rather feedback from those you trust for their candor, not their sycophancy. Remember that not all complaints are valid and not all customers are equal.

- Recognize mistakes early and cut your losses. Apologize personally for errors, search for cause and not blame, and never try to cover anything up.
- Build on your esteem to recognize that you deserve success, you've earned the rewards and perquisites of your position, and you're the best candidate for your current job or some future job, not an imposter.

Fear Factor

The way we talk to ourselves informs our behavior and is the most influential and powerful conversation we have throughout any one day.

They say there is no zealot like the converted. People who originally oppose you become more ardent supporters when they change their minds and follow you than those who were always supporters. Think of Paul on the road to Damascus, moving from a persecutor of Christians to become an Apostle and the greatest chronicler of Jesus and Christianity.

I'm recommending you commandeer this dynamic and, instead of eliminating the guy on your shoulder, use him as a zealous convert to a stronger future. This might sound bizarre for a fearless leader, but we all know that our most powerful and influential conversations every day take place within our heads.

Self-talk is influenced by our subconscious, and is revelatory. I'm suggesting you become far more consciously competent in its use, and the "little guy" is my metaphor.

- Instead of blaming yourself for things that go wrong, take credit for things that go right and things that go wrong which you correct or ameliorate.

- Stop expecting the worst and allow logic to create a better, more positive balance. Prepare to exploit success, not merely deal with catastrophe.
- Move from seeing the world as a dichotomy (black and white, up and down, left and right, correct and incorrect) and see it as a rheostat rather than a simplistic switch. Find the middle ground upon which you can negotiate and influence.

Use the guy on your shoulder to seek humor in order to reduce stress and gain perspective. Be honest about your feelings and deal with them, don't simply focus on what you "think" but also on what you're feeling.

Case Study

My son didn't get the lead role in *The Grapes of Wrath* in his senior year at the drama conservatory at the University of Miami. He was crushed, and he called me.

"How can I help?" I asked.

"Tell me how I should feel about it," he said.

"How do you feel right now?"

"I feel crushed, betrayed, resentful, and shocked."

"Well, that's how you should feel. Your feelings are always valid."

There was a moment of silence and an exhalation of breath. Then I said, "The point now is what you *do* about how you feel. You can complain to the dean, boycott the play, change your major, or simply take another role and do the best you can."

My son took another role and realized the lead wouldn't have been appropriate for him. He simply wanted his feelings validated. And he learned that it's how you handle feelings with your behavior that counts.

Allow that voice to provide ongoing positive support and confirmation of your actions, and to enable you to seek out others who will be supportive and of a kindred spirit. You and I know what we're talking about here: The guy on your shoulder is simply the representation of your self-image and self-esteem. We need to instantiate him to reach the point of this book:

Fearless leadership is about overcoming your own fears and insecurities in your life, your relationships, and your career. It is about moving boldly and quickly. It entails the drive for success and the resilience to bounce back. It's about prudent risk in a volatile world.

But basically, it's about you. The question I ask every coaching client at the moment is: Are you having fun, enjoying life?

And the question I ask every coaching client about the future is: Who do you want to be?

Once you determine who it is you want to be and how you want to be seen by others, let the guy tell you every day how you're doing and how to continue to be fearless.

In other words, keep telling yourself how good you are.

Resources

Beard, Myron, and Weiss, Alan: *The DNA of Leadership: Creating Healthy Leaders and Vibrant Organizations* (BEP, 2018).

Bennis, Warren: *The Unconscious Conspiracy: Why Leaders Can't Lead* (Wiley, 1997).

Berger, Jonah: *Invisible Influence: The Hidden Forces That Shape Behavior* (Simon & Schuster, 2017).

Citrin, Richard, and Weiss, Alan: *The Resilience Advantage: Stop Managing Stress and Find Your Resilience* (BEP, 2016).

Gardner, John: *On Leadership* (Free Press, 1993).

Goldsmith, Marshall: *What Got You Here Won't Get You There: How Successful People Become Even More Successful* (Hachette, 2014).

Goldsmith, Marshall, and Weiss, Alan: *Lifestorming: Creating Meaning and Achievement in Your Career and Life* (Wiley, 2017).

Pink, Danielle: *Drive: The Surprising Truth about What Motivates Us* (Riverhead, 2009).

Seligman, Martin: *Learned Optimism: How to Change Your Mind and Your Life* (Random House, 2006).

Talib, Nassim, and Ochman, Joe: *Antifragile: Things That Gain from Disorder* (Penguin/Random House, 2014).

Weiss, Alan: *The Unofficial Guide to Power Managing* (IDG, 2000).

Weiss, Alan: *Live Balance: How to Convert Professional Success into Personal Happiness* (Pfeiffer, 2008).

Self-Test

Please go to the web address alanweiss.com/fearlesstest and enter the code 012020 and you can take a brief test to assess your fearlessness (or fear). The results will be sent by return email and include a comparison to all others taking the test.

About the Author

Alan Weiss is one of those rare people who can say he is a consultant, speaker, and author and mean it. His consulting firm, Summit Consulting Group, Inc., has attracted clients such as Merck, Hewlett-Packard, GE, Mercedes-Benz, State Street Corporation, Times Mirror Group, The Federal Reserve, The New York Times Corporation, Toyota, and over 500 other leading organizations. He has served on the boards of directors of the Trinity Repertory Company, a Tony-Award-winning New England regional theater, Festival Ballet where he is President of the Board of Directors, and chaired the Newport International Film Festival. He has served on the Board of Governors of the Harvard Medical School Center for Mental Health and the Media.

He is an inductee into the Professional Speaking Hall of Fame® and the concurrent recipient of the National Speakers Association Council of Peers Award of Excellence, representing the top 1% of professional speakers in the world. He has been named a Fellow of the Institute of Management Consultants, one of only two people in history holding both those designations. He has written more books on consulting than anyone else.

His prolific publishing includes over 500 articles and 64 books, including his best-seller, *Million Dollar Consulting* (from McGraw-Hill). His most recent before this one are *Million Maverick*, *Lifestorming* (with Marshall Goldsmith), and *Threescore and More*. His books have been on the curricula at Villanova, Temple University, UC Berkeley, and the Wharton School of Business, and have been translated into 15 languages.

He is the recipient of the Lifetime Achievement Award of the American Press Institute, the first-ever for a non-journalist, and one of only seven awarded in the 65-year history of the association. CNBC ran a profile of his career calling him "The CEO Whisperer."

Alan has been married to the lovely Maria for 51 years, and they have two children and twin granddaughters. They reside in East Greenwich, Rhode Island, with their dogs, Coco and Bentley, a white German Shepherd.

You can acquire free text, audio, and video materials at Alan's site, alanweiss.com, as well as access his blog, Contrarian Consulting, and his podcast, The Uncomfortable Truth.

Index

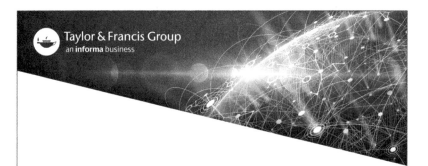

Taylor & Francis Group
an **informa** business

Taylor & Francis eBooks

www.taylorfrancis.com

A single destination for eBooks from Taylor & Francis
with increased functionality and an improved user
experience to meet the needs of our customers.

90,000+ eBooks of award-winning academic content in
Humanities, Social Science, Science, Technology, Engineering,
and Medical written by a global network of editors and authors.

TAYLOR & FRANCIS EBOOKS OFFERS:

A streamlined
experience for
our library
customers

A single point
of discovery
for all of our
eBook content

Improved
search and
discovery of
content at both
book and
chapter level

REQUEST A FREE TRIAL
support@taylorfrancis.com

Routledge
Taylor & Francis Group

CRC Press
Taylor & Francis Group